Also by R. D. Laing

The Divided Self
Self and Others
Interpersonal Perception
(with H. Phillipson and A. R. Lee)
Reason and Violence
(with David Cooper)
Sanity, Madness and the Family
(with Aaron Esterson)
The Politics of Experience
Knots
The Politics of the Family

R. D. Laing

THE FACTS OF LIFE

Allen Lane

First published in the United States of America by Pantheon Books, Inc. 1976

Published in Allen Lane 1976

ALLEN LANE
Penguin Books Ltd,
17 Grosvenor Gardens, London SW1W 0BD

ISBN 0 7139 10151

Set in Monotype Rockwell
Printed in Great Britain by
Lowe & Brydone Printers Limited, Thetford, Norfolk

Contents

For Jutta

Who knows
if life is not death,
and death life?

Euripides

Preface

We stand, sit, walk, lie down. We live in space and time and see, hear, touch, taste, smell, and sense one another, other creatures, and situations. We remember, think, imagine, look (with any or all of our senses), feel, act, talk, meet one another, reflect, wonder, doubt, believe or disbelieve, love or hate, carry on or give up.

I know that there are many who feel much the same as I do about much of what I've written about, but that there are many who may find much of it scandalous and preposterous. I've tried to *describe*, even my justifications. I've tried to portray, to depict, to display feelings, memories, observations, speculations about our life cycle, life before birth and birth, suffering and the repression of suffering. Joy and love, sex and death are hardly mentioned, but are not forgotten.

I needed to be surprised to find how difficult it was to write this book.

> *Aunque sepa los caminos*
> *Yo nunca llegaré a Cordoba**
>
> Lorca

R. D. Laing
London, 1975

* Although I may know the roads, I will never arrive at Cordoba.

Prologue

I was born at 17.15 hours on 7 October 1927, into a family that consisted of my mother and father, living in a small three-room flat on the south side of Glasgow. My father could not admit to anyone for several days that I was born.

My mother went into 'a decline'. A woman was brought in to nurse me who after six weeks turned out to be a drunken slut and another woman was brought in. She was a drunken slut as well. Then my mother took over. When I was ten months old, her mother and my mother's younger sister came to stay in our house, my mother's father having died sometime earlier, shortly before I was conceived, I surmise. Around the corner from us my father's father and my father's younger brother and younger sister lived together. His mother had died. My father was the oldest of two brothers and two sisters.

My mother was the second youngest of three sisters and two brothers. My father was the only one in his family to marry and, with one possible exception, the only one ever to commit sexual intercourse. I was the only grandchild on my father's side of the family, and the first of three cousins on my mother's side.

On my mother's side of the family, there were two older brothers and an older sister, then herself, and then a younger sister. One of her older brothers had gone off to Australia considerably before I was conceived, and there one cousin younger than me exists whom I've met only once; her older sister had one child, a boy three months younger than I. For my first four years I think he was the only child who ever entered our house, once or twice a year.

From as far back as I can remember, I tried to figure out what was going on between these people. If I believed one, I couldn't believe anyone else. Especially at the time when my mother, my mother's mother, and my mother's younger sister were all part of the same household – from ten months to eighteen months – I could not believe all of them, one of them, or none or them, entirely.

I was not allowed out alone until my first day at school. It was almost insufferably delightful. All those creatures like me to play with. And *girls* as well! When my cousin came with his mother, once or twice a year, we fought, as was expected of both of us. We 'went' around the corner once a year, at New Year's time, to see my father's father, and my father's younger brother and youngest sister came around to our house. My father's sister very occasionally came by, my father's brother once a month or so, my father's uncle once every three months or so, my father's father never. His visits ended sometime between my conception and birth.

My father regarded his father as having murdered his mother 'systematically' over the years. The last time he 'ever set foot in the door of our house' (according to my parents), the radio was on; he sat down and told my mother to turn it off. My father told my mother to do nothing of the kind. Old Pa, as my father's father was called, told my mother to turn it off. And so on. Eventually my father said, 'This is my house, and the radio will stay on unless I say so!' Old Pa said, 'Don't you speak to your father like that!' My father said, 'Get up and get out!' Old Pa reminded him once more whom he was speaking to. My father pointed out he knew very well whom he was speaking to, that was why he was telling him to get up and get out. Old Pa made no move, whereupon my father went to throw him out 'by the scruff of the neck'. The fight was on. Old Pa in his fifties, my father in his thirties. The fight went on all over the house. Eventually my father pinned Old Pa on his back across the bed, and smashed him across the face until blood was flowing. He then dragged him to the bathroom, rolled him into the bath, turned the cold water on him, heaved him out drenched with blood and water, dragged him to the door, kicked him out, and threw his cap after him. Then he stood at the window and waited to see how he would

manage to stagger or crawl away. 'He held himself up very
well,' Dad said. 'You've got to hand it to him.'

My father's younger brother, Uncle Jack, who my
parents always said had gone daft with heat stroke in China
during the First World War when he was seventeen, lived
with Old Pa, and took Old Pa's side. For several years after
the above incident, he'd come around to the house. He'd
knock on the door. He'd be let in. Not a word would be
spoken. He would take his cap off and his jacket, keeping on
his vest; he never rolled up his sleeves. My mother would
push the furniture to the side and get out of the room quickly.
I went behind the curtains. Then he and Dad would go at it.

How many times did that fight take place?
Each fight ended when Uncle Jack was down on the floor,
couldn't get up, and called enough. My mother felt sorry for
him; sometimes she would give him a cup of tea, and he
would sometimes give me half a crown before he took himself
off.

The other person who came to the house was Wee
Johnny. He was my father's uncle though they were the same
age, the son of my father's mother's mother's sister. Wee
Johnny was a perfectly formed midget. He had a perfectly
formed bowler hat and a perfectly formed three-piece suit,
and perfectly made shirts and ties, and a watch chain, even a
midget-sized umbrella, perfectly rolled. He worked as a clerk
in a linoleum factory. He climbed a small ladder up to his
perch there. When Old Pa really wanted to stir it up, he would
say that the reason Wee Johnny was so wee was because his
mother, my father's grandmother's sister, had been imbibing
gin all the time that she was pregnant and when she was
breastfeeding him. As a result, he almost drowned in gin
before he was born, and imbibing more gin than milk after, he
never grew, and that showed what that side of the family
was like.

One of my father's sisters used to tell a story
about her and Wee Johnny to gain our sympathy for her. She
once, for the first and last time, took Wee Johnny for an outing
in Edinburgh. As they were walking along Princes Street, she
became so embarrassed to be seen with him; people would
think she 'had something to do with' a midget. She started to

walk faster, and faster. To keep up with her, he started to run, bowler hat, umbrella, and all. She broke into a sprint, he ran as fast as he could, but she got away and onto a train straight back to Glasgow, leaving him, as far as she was concerned, still running up and down Princes Street trying to find her.

I remember the word 'fuck' being used in our house only once, employed by myself, at age fifteen in some such expression as 'Who does he fuckin' well think he is.' I still had no idea to what the term referred. My mother was standing in front of one of those floral designed wallpapers when the word impinged on her. Her face drained ash white, she slumped against the wall and slithered slowly to the floor. My father was so aghast he forgot to hit me, but managed to say in a quivering voice, 'Never, never, never use that word in this house again!'

It wasn't until I was seventeen that I entered a house with a stair inside and its own front door. For years I harboured the ambition of living in a house that had a stair inside it. I went to a boy's grammar school where there were no girls. At the age of sixteen, I still had no idea about what we now call the facts of life. . .

1   Primary Data

We embrace not only the absent, but those who have been, and those who *are not yet* [my italics].
'Of Vanity'*

. . . whoever shall call to memory how many and many times he has been mistaken in his own judgement, is he not a great fool if he does not ever suspect it? . . . to learn that a man has said or done a foolish thing is nothing: a man must learn that he is nothing but a fool, a much more ample and important instruction.
'Of Experience'

The advice to everyone, 'to know themselves', should be of important effect, since that god of wisdom and light caused it to be written on the front of his temple, as comprehending all he had to advise us. Plato says also, that prudence is no other thing than the execution of this ordinance; and Socrates minutely verifies it in Xenophon. The difficulties and obscurity are not discerned in any science but by those who get into it; for a certain degree of intelligence is required to be able to know that a man know not, and we must push against a door to know whether it be bolted against us or no: whence the Platonic subtlety springs, that 'neither they who know are to inquire, for as much as they know; nor they who do not know, for as much as to inquire they must know what they inquire of.' So in this, 'of knowing a man's self', that everyman is seen so resolved and satisfied with himself, that everyman thinks himself sufficiently intelligent, signifies that

* Here and below from William Hazlitt, (ed.) Charles Cotton (trans.), *Essays of Montaigne*, Navarre Society, London, 1903.

everyone knows nothing about the matter; as Socrates gives
Euthydemus to understand. I, who profess nothing else, therein
find so infinite a depth and variety, that all the fruit I have
reaped from my learning serves only to make me sensible
how much I have to learn.
'Of Experience'

*Il y a des gens qui n'auraient jamais été
amoureux, s'ils n'avaient jamais entendu parler de l'amour.*
La Rochefoucauld,
Maxim 136

(There are those who would never have loved,
had they never heard speak of love.)

My parents and I lived in a three-room flat.
My mother and I slept in one room in separate
beds, and my father slept in another room.
According to both of them, all sexual activity had
ceased between them irrevocably before I was conceived.
My mother and father still swear they do not
know how I was conceived.
But there is a birthmark on his right knee and one
on mine. A fact against immaculate conception.

When I was nine, one Saturday afternoon when I
was accompanying my mother while she was doing errands on
Victoria Road I asked her:

Ronald	where do babies come from?
Mummy	from heaven
Ronald	I know that. But how do they get here?
Mummy	their mummy and daddy pray to God to send them one
Ronald	and how is one sent?
Mummy	you'll learn that when you're older
Ronald	why can't you tell me now?
Mummy	you're too young to learn that. You'll learn that when you grow up.

That was that.

When I was fifteen, a boy in my class (in an all-male grammar school in Glasgow) drew a picture on our classroom blackboard, during the lunch interval. It was a foetus inside a womb.

Someone had once drawn a vagina on the blackboard in another classroom, and one boy in our class had once even drawn a penis. Thus far dirty drawings had gone. But this was a quantum leap farther. This was not dirt. This was filth. There were a few really dirty boys known to be in the school, two even in our class. But for sheer filth, this boy was henceforth in a class by himself.

One morning when I was sixteen my mother told me my father would have a talk about the facts of life with me when he came home from work that day. So I was waiting for him. He was late. As soon as he came in they exchanged glances. After he had taken his coat off, he came in the room, and said:

'It's time to have a talk.
I think you had better leave us, Amelia.'

This was one of the few times I can remember him addressing my mother by her first name, and about the only time I can remember her dutifully and promptly complying. She left the room immediately.

We sat down.

Dad	about the facts of life . . .
Me	Dad, it's all right. I've learned about them at school. (What a relief)
	(This was the first lie I had told for, as far as I can remember, over eight years.
	I was terrified he would try to tell me. I didn't know what they were, but I did not want to hear them from him.
	And by now I was so sorry for him I wanted to spare him the ordeal.)
Dad	O well, that's fine, that's fine. Is there anything you want to ask me?

Me	No Dad I don't think so.
Dad	Well, if you ever want to ask me anything, remember I'm your dad.
Me	I will. Thanks very much Dad.
	He had given me a book to read a few weeks back.
Dad	Did you read the book? (A stern tract against 'Self-abuse'. I could not imagine what that was.)
Me	Yes yes I did very good book very sound very sound
Dad	I've always led a clean life myself, Ronald, and I've never regretted it.
	I hope you will lead a clean life.
Me	I'll do my best.
Dad	Your mother has never had anything to complain about on that score with me.
Me	(mutter)
Dad	I learned respect for women from *my* mother.

When I was sixteen, a three-page circular was distributed among the Christian boys in my school, of whom I was counted as one, by 'The Boss' (a Church of Scotland minister, who specialized in converting Glasgow grammar school boys when they were ripe for the Lord at puberty). It drew our attention to the fact that a number of Christian boys had started to take lessons in modern ballroom dancing, namely, slow waltz, quick step, and slow fox-trot.

It pointed out that in modern ballroom dancing, contrary to Scottish country dances, and other dances, the whole of the fronts of the bodies of the dancers, who were of opposite sex, came into contact, albeit through layers of clothing.

Specifically, the breasts of the female come into contact with the chest of the male, and the genital regions of both might be pressed against each other, or at least be jostled together on a dance floor.

Even if a Christian boy held his partner at some distance from him, on a dance floor it was not possible to ensure such contact did not occur, inadvertently.

Some Christian boys might argue that they were learning ballroom dancing as a social accomplishment. They had to consider what 'social accomplishment' might mean in Sodom and Gomorrah. In a god-fearing society one might speak of 'social accomplishments', but this world was condemned as evil, given over to the Prince of Darkness. Other Christian boys argued that it was for the exercise. We were reminded that there were other healthy ways of taking exercise.

We also had to consider what sort of girls and women went in for ballroom dancing. Would a modern dance hall be the place a Christian boy would go, expecting to meet a Christian girl?

No. If a boy was honest, he would have to admit that ballroom dancing was undertaken because of *sex*. Jesus Christ had died on the Cross for our sins, a fact that should not be forgotten for one moment. Could one, with a good conscience, dance a slow fox-trot, and remember, at the same time, the crucifixion?

The Boss said he would not condemn ballroom dancing outright. It was unnecessary. We should pray about it, and ask God for guidance. The Boss had no doubt what that guidance would be.

In the Sixth Form, I think some of the boys 'knew' or guessed, but I never heard the matter discussed, and I can remember only one conversation I had on the subject.

My closest friend at the time was eighteen, I was seventeen. We were both beginning to read Greek fairly fluently. We had both read chunks of Homer, Sophocles, Aeschylus, Plato . . .

He confided in me that his mother had just had a talk with him. She told him that he was going to have a baby brother or sister in about two weeks' time. He was flabbergasted.

His mother further indicated to him that the baby was *inside her stomach*.

Come to think of it, she was rather more stout, but it had never crossed his mind that there was a baby inside his mother's stomach (by stomach he meant abdomen – the common word for abdomen in these parts was stomach, the same word as for the organ of that name).

I did not venture to inquire if he had asked or had been told how the baby got there, but my assumption was (and it is still my surmise) that he had no *idea* whatever how he or she got there.

No one ever told me 'the facts of life'.

I looked up the sections under Sex and Reproduction in the Encyclopaedia Britannica in my local public library, but the most relevant pages were actually worn away, and where not, so faded and smudged as to be illegible.

I dared not ask the librarian. It took all my courage to consult these pages in the reference section without being caught.

What if one of my teachers had come in? Or one of the boys at school? and looked over my shoulder at what I was reading! Or just asked me, 'What are you looking up?'

I looked through the biggest respectable bookshop in town, Smiths on St Vincent Street, but could find nothing. Eventually I went to the book section of the largest most anonymous department store, found a book on the dangers of venereal disease, with explicit illustrations – I had now established, just before my sixteenth birthday, that men put their penises into a thing called a vagina, which women have but men do not have. Then they 'ejaculate', which results in something coming out of the penis, called semen, and this goes right inside the woman's body. This semen contains sperm, so small they cannot be seen and one of them . . .

2   Speculation

I was twelve before I discovered I had not been the first child to ask these age-old questions. What a consolation that was!

When did 'I' begin? When do 'I' end?
What am I? Am I?

By what criteria shall I answer these questions?
By what criteria shall I scrutinize these questions,
to decide whether or not they are answerable?

For as long as I can remember I was trying to figure out how I got here, what was I doing here, why was I here, why were other people here.

I questioned the here, when, and what we were in. But my own most immediate, urgent, concern was what I and we *were*. What are we doing here? What are we *supposed* to be doing here? Where is here?

Did I come from anywhere?
Am I going to anywhere?

Are there people who know more about these matters than I?

Are we all essentially, equally ignorant?
but some are more ignorant than others, ignorant of their ignorance, hence thinking they know?

Is there any sense in wondering
who or what I am and why I am here?

Did I begin before or after, or at, the conception
of the first cell of me?
Shall I end before or after, or at, my death?

Am I dead or alive?
Am I asleep or awake?
How can I be certain this is not a dream?
How do I know whether my world is not a
five-channel synchronized hallucination?

I don't think I ever thought
I was the I that thinks it's me

When it disappears
the I that sees
I am no longer here nor there
is an I
I cannot see
but only be

My Face

I see it in the mirror
I take the mirror image, turning it round, and
place it in the space where it is now suspended,
between 'me', and the paper I am writing upon.

I take off this visual mask, an inverted reversed
image of a reflection.

What is my face now?

There are different kinds of 'feelings' in the
space where the mask was.

The more I concentrate on them the more porous
they become – they fade and dissolve into
finer and finer dust.

I thought I had a face.

We look into a brain, we do not see the sky,
we see only brain.

Looking at my head in a mirror
I infer that if I opened up my skull
there I would see a brain.

I believe if my visual cortex were destroyed
my visual world would disappear
if different parts of my brain were destroyed
I would lose my sense of sound
         sense of taste
         sense of touch
         sense of smell
         sense of sight
and all the other known powers of my mind.

Does this mean that 'I' would not be able to
propel the vehicle of my body because it was so damaged I
could no longer use it?

If it did not seem to be the case, how could I
begin to imagine that this universe is the
experience of this collection of grizzle, tendons,
blood, bone, neural tissue, etc., etc., this colony
of billions of cells (of different sorts), all
the descendants of one cell?

The first cell of me carried within it
all the resources needed to become, given the
precise environment I actually have had, precisely
what I actually now am.

What an extraordinary arrangement to be?

We would think it were impossible, but for the
fact that it seems to be.

I am the outcome of the way my genetic system,
carried in one cell, has reacted, given the environment it and
its descendants, whom I often call me, have encountered.
The fact that I am writing this, thinking these
thoughts, etc., is the outcome of this interplay from the very
first cell of me.

Physically,

my body appears to be
a physical system of certain ways of its own,
a part of the physical world, the domain of
physics.
What is the domain of physics? The physical
world.

Opinions differ greatly on this among physicists.

It is very difficult, perhaps in principle impos-
sible, for us to *define* the physical world, to set its limits and
limitations, since our brains, without which such speculations,
I suppose, are impossible, are themselves elements, I take it,
of the physical world.

My brain infers from this world it *sees*, etc., that
it is all, including itself, a transform *into* phenomena *of* physical
events occurring *in* itself.

These physical events occurring in my visual
cortex are completely unseen by me, while I am seeing what
I am seeing. Nor do they *look* like what 'I' am seeing. Yet
without them, I would see nothing.

The physical transforms in our bodies, in and
from the eye through further transforms in and through nerves
and synapses to further transforms in the brain, seem to be the
sine qua non of vision. Yet they do not appear to resemble the
world: or even distal objects out there. What are we seeing?
We cannot be sure we are seeing what we *suppose* is out
there, whatever we suppose. Nor can we be sure even that
we see some sort of copy, or picture, of what we suppose is
out there. If it comes to that, we cannot be certain that there *is*
anything out there apart from what we see. Suppose the mind,
a non-physical X, uses the brain as its instrument. When the
brain is destroyed bit by bit the instrument is destroyed bit
by bit.

I am told my brain is like a camera. It takes
pictures. The world is the brain's three-dimensional movie
made out of millions of stills per second.

But my brain is itself a part of the picture.
What is my brain a picture of?

My visual head is itself a very small part of my
visual world. Therefore my head is only a very small part of
what is in it.

All my inferences as to how my visual world
comes to be here, as transform of transforms of transforms . . .,
derive from the last of these inferred transforms, namely, the
visual world.

> let Z = the phenomenal world
> let A = non-phenomenal

All the transforms except the presumptive last one
are non-phenomenal, the distal stimulus (the first) being the
most remote.

Not until, at, or after the neural events subtending
vision (and all phenomena), does vision (and all phenomena)
occur. The visual cortex is itself a visual object. The visual
cortex is itself a member of the class of visual objects, which
comprise the last transform.

Therefore the visual cortex as a visual object
cannot be used to account for its own visual existence since it
is itself an object of vision (a member of set Z).

This would be to suggest that a photograph of a
camera took the photograph.

What I see is an event that occurs when something happens
in my visual cortex.
No intact optical system, no sight.
The optical system is a *conditio sine qua non* of vision,
as far as I infer.

People without an intact optical system are blind.
And so for all organs of sense and sensibility.

A distal stimulus generates a pattern of energy
which is transmitted across a distance. These energy transforms undergo further transforms into transforms of neural
energy and after many adventures of transforms of transforms
of transforms along nerves across synaptic junctions, transforms occur in the visual cortex the outcome of which is my
visual world.

Is my visual world in my head?

Is my world in my head?
The visual apparatus is destroyed:
I am blind
? I can't take pictures any more?

If my physical frame dissolves, I can't live in this
world any more, because this world is a transform: the brain is the transformer and is itself a
transform.

When we look at a brain,
how could we guess that
the sky, earth, whole world
is a transform of the physical
processes that go on in it

but the brain is itself a transform
of what?

There is the world of phenomena (Z).
Without, I infer, a domain of non-phenomenal
physical events (A → Y),
the world of phenomena would not exist.
At every point in every detail the world I am sure
of is subtended by and *totally* at the mercy of
what I can only infer.

The inference I am forced to make from the
evidence is that the evident (Z) is a manifestation
of the unmanifest (A). Shall I call the physical
world both manifest and unmanifest?
Is the phenomenal world a transformation of the
physical world?
or is there *no* physical world except the
phenomenal?
Do we banish from the physical world, even, the
phenomenal world, all we are aware of actually,
and infer only therefrom, that only the inferred
world is physical?

The distal stimulus is not a phenomenon since it
never happens in the visual cortex
hence
the distal stimulus of the phenomenal visual
cortex cannot be happening *in* the phenomenal
visual cortex.

How can I be in my brain if the brain is part of
the picture *of* me?

The actual me of whom the picture is a picture
can hardly be *in* the picture. Surely *in* the picture can only be
a *picture of* me.

Maybe the picture I have of myself is only the
part of the picture that can be seen in itself. But I cannot see
myself. This does not mean I am not part of the picture. But a
picture of whom, of what, and who sees the picture?

If 'I' can be said to 'be' at all, I cannot be only a
picture of nothing.

This collection of cells has the impression that it
is I. This is a proposition I do not necessarily agree with.

It is generally thought by neuroscientists that the
collection of cells called my body, especially that collection
that makes up my central nervous system, receives input,
processes it, and the *output* of this sensory processing is the
phenomenal universe we live in.

Since everything we know, including ourselves,
is part of the transform, we can never expect to know as
transforms what we are transforms of.

Or maybe we are footprints. Michelangelo compared himself to God's footprint in the mud.

The brain is one of the set of phenomenal objects.

How, as a member of the set we have to account
for, can it be used to account for the set as a whole, and all
members of the set, including itself?

3   Nature and Nurture

I take it on the authority of biologists that, biologically speaking, we all have begun in the same way.

Namely, as one cell, somewhere in one of the uterine tubes, or in the womb of one's mother.

This one cell is the outcome of the union of two cells, one from one's mother, the ovum, and one from one's father, a sperm.

The advent of that one cell was the beginning of that collection of cells which without exception are the cellular descendants of that one cell. I, as I write this, biologically speaking am a collection of cells (in the order of 2^{64+}, they tell me), all of which count one cell, forty-eight years ago, as our common ancestor.

Moreover, I am told that the first one of me, in dividing and dividing, had, at the moment of its conception, the same genetic structure (with a few exceptions) as every one of the 2^{64} of me has now.

This one cell is the cell all my cells are derived from, by a process of it dividing into two, each of these two dividing into a further two, and so on, and on.

However it's a moot point whether this precise knowledge of our microscopic origin and growth into the macroscopic domain changes or settles finally any of the basic philosophical problems attendant on the question 'Who am I?'

For as early as I remember I never took my self to *be* what people called me. That at least has remained crystal clear to me. That is, whatever, whoever I may be is not to be confused with the names people give *to* me, or how they *describe* me, or what they *call* me. I am not my name.

Who or what I am as far as they are concerned, is not necessarily, or thereby, *me*, as far as I am concerned.

I am presumably *what* they are describing, but not their description. I am the territory, what they say I am is their map of me.

And what I call myself to myself is, presumably, my map of me. What, o where, is the territory?

I accept, provisionally, as fact that my biological being will end with the dissolution, dispersal, destruction of this collection of cells as a coherent system.

These cells of me will keep going together perhaps a little longer. This present arrangement of cells does not seem to know consciously for how long but we have concluded that we are not going on forever in our present arrangement as a human body. We, it, I, they, will, as they say, die.

This collection of 2^{64} and beyond divisions of one cell is unable to find a satisfactory resolution to a number of aspects of its own attempts to analyse itself.

This collection is aware of communications from other collections. Some of these other collections are reported to have stated that we are indeed temporary arrangements, and that like all other arrangements, our sort dissolves. Some collections seem to feel that a sad thought, some are relieved.

Am 'I' no more or less than this collection?
Shall I pass away when it passes away?
How can I tell?
Revelations and opinions differ.
One man's revelation is another's anathema.
There is no consensus.
There is not even a consensus among collections similar to me, or mine, that we are alive. Some collections have concluded that they are dead. Some have concluded that we are ghosts, we die at conception, and will be conceived into life when we 'die'. Who can say? Who can say whether we are alive or dead?

We are physical systems who, by our own experience, are *sentient*. We feel.

Without the necessary physical arrangements there might be, for all I am aware of knowing, no consciousness either. How can I tell if there would be a me, even?

The physical arrangements which apparently subtend my consciousness and my world yield no consciousness of that world if they cannot function in very precise ways.

The continued existence of such functions seems to depend on appropriate physical environmental cirumstances.

My sentience is not necessary to my immediate physical survival.

I can be physically alive, and yet be anaesthetic, heartless, insensible, and virtually mindless.

We seem to be like all other living physical systems.

We flourish under certain circumstances, and we wilt under others.

It seems then that a healthy human being possessed of motility would have a tropism for its optimizing environment.

It seems that we have a tendency in the *opposite* direction.

A tendency actually to *create*, and to live in by choice, minimizing environments, and to seek to normalize our environment at far short of optimum.*

G = the genetic system
E = its environment

Am I a product of G and E? Am I G?
G's immediate cellular environment is my body.
My body, except G, is non-G.
G is at present thought to remain almost unchanged by its expectable environment.

* For instance, when I was in Honolulu recently (1973), there was an international conference on the environment convened and attended by 'environmentalist freaks', we heard, who are now arguing that everyone is entitled to 'super-pure air'!

Nature and Nurture

As G receives information from E, my body, G reacts as the necessity of its arrangements dictate, and E responds likewise, and so on, until G can find no further responses consonant with it and its cytoplasmic E associates continuing together in the form we call ourselves.

From the beginning (conception) to the end (death)
of the life cycle is E

plus or minus in relation to G?
for or against G?
do I want
more or less of it?
is E safe or dangerous?
does E *welcome* me or spurn me?
is it friendly or hostile?

The *first* environment of G *must be*

plus or minus to G
etc. etc.

E *must* react to G, as G *must* react to E.

The *ovum* is washed away. No *unfertilized ovum* ever implants. Implantation is to be *adopted.*

The earth is my mother. My mother was my earth.

The *power* I had as *one* cell to affect my environment I shall never have again.

Does E welcome or reject G?
Does G come as friend or foe?

G reacts to physical fields in E that we are only beginning to glimpse.

G is exposed to all radiation effects, electromagnetic fields of local and cosmic physico-molecular-chemical energy forces. This is all our basic environmental matrix; if that changes just, to us, a very little, in some directions, in no time we may be dead, or genetically wounded for life.

Our genetic system directs our response system to E. It must be the case that there are many types of E's at every stage of our life, whether as one cell or billions, but basically, they are plus or minus, for me or against me.

The environment is registered from the very beginning of my life: by the first one of me. What happens to the first one or two of me may reverberate throughout all subsequent generations of our first cellular parents. That first one of us carries *all* my 'genetic' memories.

Our first experience of this universe occurs within a uterine tube in a female human body.

How many conceptions are desired?

How many of us are desired *only* for conception, but not to be adopted by implantation? How many of us might have been better to take no for an answer then?

How many never implant? How many abort spontaneously? How many are aborted? How many abortions fail? How many miscarriages fail?

Of those that come to birth,
how many have been desired all the way,
wholeheartedly from conception to birth,
how many are born because

(i)   they were conceived unintentionally,

(ii)   or implanted despite attempts to prevent them

(iii)   attempts (mental and/or physical) at abortion
           failed,

(iv)   though abortion not attempted,
           mentally or physically,
           it was fervently prayed for,
           and the prayers went unanswered

(v)   abortion desired
           but attempts inhibited by guilt, shame, fear?

If the women who have answered me are to be believed, the usual, the (statistical) 'norm' is to have been *unwanted*.

There were many fewer abortions in the years
up to, say, 1965 than in the last few years.

It seems that although people were more careful
to avoid misconceptions in those days, because abortions were
more difficult to have and much more morally condemned,
many of us must have been conceived against our parents'
desires and hung on in a womb through perhaps both
conscious and unconscious attempts to destroy us before or
after implantation.

The difference between being welcome and
unwelcome, between a welcoming environment and an
unwelcoming environment, is all the difference in the world.
Even to enter a room. The difference between being welcomed or not welcomed!

We cannot take the life cycle of the *wanted* as the
statistical norm.

What sort of reception awaits each new arrival
(zygote)? May yes or no from E at this stage (zygote) reverberate through all the generations of that first one of us all?

Can E *lie* at the beginning?

E influences G from the very beginning. It takes
unusual influences to alter G itself, but G and non-G act, react
all the time. Am I that interaction?

I suppose that all non-G in and around G does
not necessarily *influence* G.

We only know whether or not the environment
influences us by noticing we are influenced. If we do not
notice we are being influenced, we cannot know we are.

We may still infer it. Some E may be of the order
that its influence is to render us unaware of its influence, in
inverse proportion to its influence, e.g. a toxic environment
may render us *insensible* to its toxicity.

Are we re-creating around us an artificial
environment which has a tendency to induce in us an
unawareness of its noxious characteristics: an anaesthetizing
noxious sublethal environment?

There are countless ways in which we can all be
killed by our environments. Some of these ways, not directly

perceived by us, we may have or may yet develop instru-
ments to detect.

      We have no way of putting a credible limit on
the ways we may be influenced for weal or woe, without
being aware that we are being thus influenced, perhaps
without even dreaming we are thus influenced.

Am I unaffected by anything?

One cannot pluck a flower
without disturbing a star,
it has been said

And if the stars are disturbed?

4   Feelings and Physics

The question I am most frequently asked in the USA is *How do we get in touch with our feelings?* Is this state of affairs the outcome of the interplay of G and E?

Feelings, dreams, you name it, may be cultured out, like the fairies, elves, goblins, water spirits, gods and goddesses, angels . . . G's response to certain environmental circumstances is, apparently, no-feeling.

Heartlessness and charity are manifested through a physical system, steered by or through G. Millions of people fear their feelings.

An American professor speaking of possible unconscious feelings: 'We'll try to catch them at the dream level and cut them off there.'

The couple, he a second-year engineering student, she a second-year humanities student, who asked: 'Should we try to get in touch with our feelings now, or wait until we graduate?'

Feelings are both feel *of*, and feel *for*. In either case feelings are now a commodity. Many people cannot afford the luxury. Experts teach how to feel either or both ways.

Heartless sentience is sensuality, the feel *of*, without feeling *for*.

People have agonized over their feelings for a long time.

'I love and I hate, and I am on the rack' (*excrucior*), wrote Catullus.

and who or what can free a man 'From eager impetuous loves;
from vain and disappointing hopes; from lawless and ex-
orbitant appetites; from frothy and empty joy; from dismal
and presaging fears and anxious cares; from inward heart
burnings; from self-eating Envy; from swelling Pride, and
Ambition; from dull and black Melancholy; from boiling
Anger, and raging Fury; from a gnawing, aiking Conscience;
from Arbitrary Presumptions; from rigid Sourness, and
Severity of Spirit: for these make the Man that is not biass'd
and principled by Religion, inwardly to boil; to be Hot with
the Fervours of Hell. . .'*

But it's all right. The fires of Hell are now under
control. They are thermostatically regulated by chemicaliza-
tion. Hell has been conquered by the industrial-medical
complex.†

Me   Can you put words to it?

She   It's everything
            it's nothing
            it's death
            the mechanical death of human beings
            a black hole
            Zero

            A mechanical man has a pump, a heartless pump.
            If the heart is a pump, show me a pump with
            a heart?
            I am told that 'Thought' is represented in
            Egyptian hieroglyphics by the image of the heart.

We feel E, and we feel toward E. How I feel
toward E is affected by how E feels. If I cannot feel E, I may
hate E or E hates me and I hate E. What's the point of feelings
anyway? Would we not be better off without them? Are
feelings being cultured out? Have they a survival value?

---

* Benjamin Whichcote, *Select Sermons* . . . , London, 1698, p.
17, quoted by Margaret L. Wiley, *Creative Sceptics,* Allen & Unwin, London, 1966.
† Ivan Illich, *Medical Nemesis,* Marion Boyars, London, 1976.

College   My feelings are way down there,
Professor   somewhere,
             I suppose,
             if they are anywhere
             I banished them years ago
             they were not worth it
             I hated my feelings
             I told them to fuck off
             and they fucked off
             I've never heard from them since
             I've not an inkling how I feel about
             anything
             I can hardly remember what
             feelings are

   Does our contemporary environment preclude
the possibility of a healthy phenotype from a healthy geno-
type?

5   Life before Birth

Stages in My Life

A	conception to implantation
B	implantation to birth
C	postnatal life
M_0	mother before conception
M_1	mother from conception to implantation
$M_{1 \cdot 1}$	mother from implantation to completion of birth
M_2	postnatal mother

One of our great tasks seems to be coming to the realization that $M_0 = M_1 = M_2$

Do we have a genetic mental map of our whole life cycle with its different phases – mental patterns which reflect biological forms and transforms?

It seems to me credible, at least, that all our experience in our life cycle from cell one is absorbed and stored from the beginning, perhaps especially in the beginning.

How that may happen, I do not know.

How can one cell generate the billions of billions of cells I now am?

We are impossible, but for the fact that we are.

When I *look* at embryological stages in my life cycle I experience what feel to me like sympathetic reverberations, vibrations in me now with how I now feel I felt then.

Photographs, illustrations, films of early embryological stages of our life cycle often move people very much.

If you were to die now,
and be reconceived tonight
which woman would you choose to spend the
first nine months of your next lifetime inside of?

That many people feel similar, and often strong,
sympathetic vibrations (resonances, reverberations) when they
unguardedly allow themselves to imagine how they might have
felt from conception to and through birth and early infancy is
a *fact*.

But what does this mean?

Is it possible for we cells,
before and after specifically neural tissue arises,
to reproduce in later phases of the life cycle
transforms, or variations, of our very first
experiences?

May our prenatal experiential patterns
function as templates
for some of the patterns
woven into the complex knit of postnatal design?

Prenatal patterns mapped onto postnatal regions
occasioning disturbances of normal postnatal
function e.g.

womb	umbilical blood	foetus	placenta
↓	↓	↓	↓
skull	thoughts	mind	brain

the person feels like a foetus in the womb of his
skull being fed by thoughts from his brain
the skull is a womb he is inside (crucified, dead
and buried),
and a placental-breast
from which he is sustained and poisoned
by thoughts (blood, milk, food)

It is at least *conceivable* to me that myths, legends, stories, dreams, fantasies, and conduct *may* contain strong reverberations of our uterine experience.

If this were so, such later affections could properly and appropriately be called *hysterical* (i.e. uterine).

Some myths fit better than others but enough do to make me consider seriously the possibility that conception to implantation, and subsequent prenatal adventures, are represented mythologically in postnatal imagery.

Mythology may be a key to our embryological experience.

There are I suspect even *greater* varieties of prenatal experiences (and of more interest and greater moment, S. T. Coleridge remarked), than there are of post-natal experiences.

'The standard saga itself may be formulated according to the following outline:

> The hero is the child of most distinguished parents,
> usually the son of a king.
>
> His origin is preceded by difficulties,
> such as continence,
> or prolonged barrenness,
> or secret intercourse of the parents due to external prohibition or obstacles.
>
> During or before the pregnancy,
> there is a prophecy,
> in the form of a dream or oracle,
> cautioning against his birth,
> and usually threatening danger to the father (or his representative).
>
> As a rule,
> he is surrendered to the water, in a box.
> He is then saved by animals,
> or by lowly people (shepherds),
> and is suckled by a female animal or by an humble woman.

After he has grown up,
he finds his distinguished parents,
in a highly versatile fashion.

He takes his revenge on his father,
on the one hand,
and is acknowledged, on the other.

Finally he achieves rank and honors.'*

Sargon was brought forth in a hidden place	conceived in uterine tube
His mother, the vestal, laid me in a vessel made of reeds	zona pellucida
closed my door with pitch and dropped me down into the river	in the uterine tube
which did not drown me	the secretions of the uterine tube, which nourish, or famish, us in the first seven and a half days before implantation, as the case may be: called by embryo- logists 'uterine milk'
The river carried him to AKKI the water carrier who lifted him up	adoption by endometrium
in the kindness of his heart He became his gardener	early implantation chorionic embryo
and then king†	mature foetus

Sargon was put in
a vessel made of reeds
the door closed with pitch
dropped me into the river
then adopted

* Otto Rank, *The Myth of the Birth of the Hero and Other Writings*,
Alfred A. Knopf, New York, 1959, p. 85.
† Rank, op. cit., p. 15.

Moses was placed in an ark
of bulrushes daubed with
slime and pitch
laid it in the flags by the
river's brink then adopted

Karne had a large basket of rushes
a lid placed thereon
lined with wax
floats on river waves
until adopted from the river

and so on

In many myths,
the hero   zygote
is put in a
container of some kind
a boat   zona pellucida
a box
a sphere
a casket
into a river   uterine canal/tube/duct
or the sea
lands on the shore   endometrium
is saved   little understood adoption
and nurtured by   of the blastocyst by the
animals or lowly people   uterine endometrium
prospers   and
becomes adopted by   grows into a foetus
the King and Queen of the city   in womb city
                          until
leaves   birth
finds after many adventures   and subsequent adventures
his real parents   in correlating M_0 with
                          M_1, M_2

He is now twenty-nine.

At age eighteen he falls in love (with girl No. 1)
He and his girl are as one
Something stirs in him
He feels imaginative, reflective, creative
It is very deep
She does not understand

He meets girl No. 2
She understands
He starts an affair with No. 2, but does not tell No. 1
He and No. 2 discuss how not to hurt No. 1
He leaves No. 1 for No. 2
for a while he feels empty
then he begins to feel something develop inside him again
it is very deep
No. 2 does not understand
he meets No. 3
No. 3 understands
he starts an affair with No. 3
he and No. 3 discuss how not to hurt No. 2
he leaves No. 2 for No. 3
nothing happens for a while
then something new begins to develop inside him
it is very deep
No. 3 is not able to comprehend
No. 4 does
he and No. 4 discuss how to break the news to No. 3
he leaves No. 3 for No. 4
he completes his first scientific paper
he feels empty
he begins to feel creative again
No. 4 does not understand
No. 5 does understand
he has an affair with No. 5
    but does not want to hurt No. 4
he knows so well how she must feel
he leaves No. 4 for No. 5

he is now in transit from No. 6 to No. 7

Reconstruction

His mother gave birth to a younger sister when he was
eighteen months old.

M_0 = M before his conception
M_1 = his mother between conception and birth
M_2 = his mother after his birth

---

1. he and his mother (M_1 M_2) are as one

    he and his girl friend are as one

---

2. his mother becomes pregnant with sister

    he starts to feel creative with deep thoughts/feelings

---

3. he does not understand what is going on inside mother

    No. 1 does not understand what is going on inside him

---

4. his mother and father discuss how not to hurt him

    he and girl No. 2 discuss how not to hurt girl No. 1
        girl No. 3 discuss how not to hurt girl No. 2
        girl No. 4 discuss how not to hurt girl No. 3

---

5. he feels his mother leaves him for his father

    he leaves girl No. 1 for girl No. 2
        leaves girl No. 2 for girl No. 3

---

6. his mother gives birth to a baby sister

    he produces a "paper"

He 'knows' what No. 1 is going through and going to go
through when he meets No. 2
because when he meets No. 2

    No. 2 = his father
    No. 1 = himself as a baby
he = his pregnant mother
        his
  scientific
    paper = the embryo inside his mother

but at the beginning
he (embryo) and girlfriend (M_1) are one
then girlfriend becomes him as baby
he becomes his mother (M_2)
the next girlfriend becomes his father

Quite a few 'heterosexual' men marry in this sense their fathers

        mother   father
          | |
          ↓   ↓
        husband   wife

slip of the tongue :

A husband   'What am I doing, marrying your fucking
to his wife   father-in-law?'

                What indeed !

The world is my womb, and my mother's womb was my first
world.

the *womb* is the first of the series
                of contexts
                  containers
                  whatever one is *in*

a room
a space
a time
a relationship
a mood

whatever is around
whoever* is felt as around me
one's atmosphere
one's *circum*stances
one's environment
the world†

Blastula

Shelley's dome of many-coloured glass that stains the white
radiance of eternity?

a geodesic dome	flying saucer
a sphere	sun-god
a balloon	football
the moon	
a space capsule	

the zygote and blastula in the zona pellucida

zona pellucida	a box		
	a casket		
	an ark		
	a swan		
uterine tube	the water	the ocean	a river

* A woman says: 'My father was *there* but he was never around.'
† 'As far as I can make out, there is never anything but womb . . .
It is failure to recognize the world as womb which is the cause of our misery, in
large part.' Henry Miller, 'The Enormous Womb', in *The Wisdom of the Heart*,
New Directions Publishing Corp., New York, 1960, p. 94.

journey along uterine tube / time in ocean, or drifting
to implantation in womb / down river, till picked up
/ by animals or shepherds, etc.
thus conception / in myths birth
uterine journey / exposure to sea or river in
/ a box or casket
implantation / adoption by animals, or
reception by / lowly people
uterine endometrium

Before Implantation

The secretions of the uterine tube may be calm or stormy

(the invisible worm that flies in the
night in the horrible storm)

plentiful or a drought

one may spin, revolve, float, fly;

be dashed against rocks;

be washed ashore and be washed away again,

before journey's end

Before eventual definitive implantation there may
be many adventures. This journey to implantation may form a
template for subsequent patterns. As implantation may be
mapped onto birth.

Implantation

Implantation may have been as horrific and as wonderful as
birth;

Reverberating through our lives, and being resonated by
experiences of being sucked in, drawn in, pulled
in, dragged down; of being rescued, revived,
succoured, welcomed; of trying to get in, but
being kept out; perishing through fatigue,
exhaustion; frantic, helpless, impotent, etc.

Images of quicksand, swamps; exposure (upon loss
of zona pellucida): then after all those possible
        storms, winds, risks of shipwreck,
        drowning; experience of
        breaking up, going to pieces,
        adoption by uterus (M_1).

The basic possibilities can be expressed in the
standard four-cell matrix

        uterus

blastula   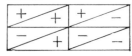

    a bed of crimson joy or a battleground

    The original template for all reception,
    entering: pushing oneself in or being pulled
    in; battling one's way in or a reciprocal embrace
    of love.*
    Does one enjoy diving fearlessly into things,
    putting feelers out (villi, fingers); exploring,
    with love or hate, a loving or hating world?

    To put my proposition succinctly: birth is
implantation in reverse and the reception one receives from
the postnatal world generates a sympathetic resonance in us
of our first adoption by our prenatal world.

        I feel
        I am
        clinging to crumbling rocks
        liable to be swept away
           in the torrent

* Freud, in *The Interpretation of Dreams, Standard Edition*,
Hogarth Press, London, 1953, vol. V, p. 400, suggests that entry dreams are birth
dreams in reverse. Jones, Rank, Fodor, and others follow him in this. If not
reversed by interpretation, these dreams are, in manifest content, implantation
dreams.

hanging on for dear life
trying to get a foothold
never seeming as though
I can get *into* what I'm doing

Always trying to get *in*
Everything glances off me
I feel in a whirl
as though I'm turning round
        and round faster and faster
and I could whirl away forever

I feel out of time
I seem to react to everything
just a few milliseconds too late
It's what I do in these milliseconds

nothing to hang onto
nothing to get my teeth into

first extensions into endometrium

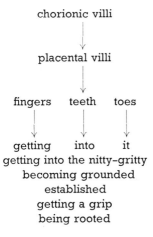

        chorionic villi

       placental villi

  fingers   teeth   toes

  getting   into   it
getting into the nitty-gritty
becoming grounded
established
getting a grip
being rooted

Chorionic Fear

I feel like a sponge. A deep underwater creature
like an anemone
    I'm sodden with terror
    suffused with fear
a terrified sponge
    I'm helpless
    I can't move   It's meaningless to get out of it by
                     running away
                     talking
    I'm quivering all over

A woman of thirty tells me of a dream.

        a piece of gum is going down an escalator
        the steps of which are not moving
                to a garage

    She had been keeping a dream book. She was
struck by this dream, of over a year back, which she had forgotten, because it occurred, she subsequently calculated, two
nights after she had conceived.
    She had not '*dreamt*' she had conceived until she
'*missed*' her next period.
    But she now wondered whether this dream could
in some way be a representation of a zygote (piece of gum)
going along the uterine tube (escalator) to the uterus (garage)?

a woman has an abortion

        she dreams a white horse bounds free
        from the narrow window of a jail

She is twenty-eight

she is terrified of   being sucked into   attracted to
                                              fascinated by
the sea
the darkness
the underworld
since a child she has had the
feeling of being a changeling:
more like a dolphin

she used to say
'If I disappear, I will have gone back to the sea
                                   to the underworld'
she has an affinity to
graveyards,
death, whirlpools
twice nearly drowned:
to the point of nearly dying

Experience of a man in his late twenties

One day, at home, he went up the stairs to the bathroom. He
blacked out. He found himself hunched on the floor 'terror-
stricken, as though in a terror-stricken box'.

              I ask myself, is it
                  possible that
       he travelled along the
                 uterine tube   stairs
          in zona pellucida   box
          and upon entering
          the uterine cavity   bathroom
             a catastrophic
     experience occurred   blackout and
                               terror-stricken
                               in a terror-stricken box

occasioning his whole being
       to be terror-stricken,

which is still reverberating
through all the cells of
his body

Miss B, age fifty

She floats, drifts, is carried along, often in a spin

but she can never find
a home   never put down roots
or make a home   never be 'earthed'.
or settle down

He is thirty-four

Dream

sliding along a road   uterine tube
near his birthplace   conception
he has an overcoat on   zona pellucida
it gets wetter   increse in secretion
                          of 'uterine milk'
he comes to an L-shaped   comes through tube into
room   uterus

he is about to go into a
building like a theatre   impending implantation
he puts one finger into the
place   first of 'villi'
where he goes in
to touch two hands (fingers)
of a clock
he sits on a throne in the
theatre   implanted
children come to him   beginning of exchange with
                          endometrial messengers
there is a problem on how establishing embryonic-
to communicate   maternal communication at
                          implantation site

She is thirty

She can remember nothing except pain and terror.

she feels like a ball of fear	blastocyst anxiety
she feels like a round sponge sodden with terror	chorionic anxiety
in dreams she sees herself like a globe spinning around	blastocyst before implantation
there is a Paisley pattern on the surface	
she is overtaken by a fear of (the globe) falling she tries desperately to procrastinate	pre-implantation anxiety
she fears she is going to be buried alive	fear of implantation
her mother and her fear tell her she has to be buried	

Miss K is a spinster. She lives alone. She is fifty-five.

She is permanently up in the air, in a whirl, dizzy, unrooted, homeless, unembedded

She travels from an island where she lives, by ferry, train, and tube, to large department stores and supermarkets.

She is continually 'sensing' things going on around.

Is she permanently
a blastula   governed by the lunar cycle   a lunatic

perpetually travelling
        in tubes, ferries   uterine tube
        trains,
    going to big stores   endometrium
but never implanting?

He feels himself to be in the stratosphere.
He needs to *enter* the world.
He works as a tube train driver.

        I noted the following when I was beginning this book. As I got more into it, the feeling passed. Every time I start to write these days I have to overcome inner resistance to doing so. It was not always like this. I used to plunge into writing as often as I could and could never do so enough. But now there is a trace of physical nausea just before sitting down to write. I sometimes pace up and down and shy away from sitting down. I can almost feel the *neighing* in my nostrils.
        Once I start (if I can bring myself to get started, which is not always) I have a run for it. Sometimes for two or three hours, when I'm in it. But I 'surface' from it, involuntarily, usually after an hour or so. Then I'm out of it. And have to make a cup of tea, or eat a slice of bread, or go out and buy a pack of cigarettes, and walk up and down, and then overcome the pull back, the nausea, the shying away, the feeling between sneezing, a running nose, and crying, and get down to it once more. Anything to do with implantation?

A businessman of thirty-six

        I feel I'm hanging onto a cliff
        with my fingernails
        if I let go, I'll float off down the river
        I'll be washed away
        I shall be completely mad

A dream of a psychotherapist

>She is walking with a very disturbed young man who has been her patient for several years. The ground is reddish, soft, wet, spongylike, sodden, sand, by the seashore. There are sudden dips and pits on the surface. She is frightened of falling in one, or of David sinking into the ground, then she sees him, in a pit, shaft, naked with an astronaut's head-dress, falling into a lake

She is past thirty

>she makes a superficial
>>impression
>but does not seem to be   arrest
>>able to go further
>cannot get *into* a scene   fixation
>>a subject   *existential stasis*
>can't get into the nitty-   at
>gritty and on through to   implantation
>>achievement

He is a professor of linguistics, aged forty-three

>>>>>where he is unknown
>he travels to a non-Western country   cannot contact anyone
>>>>>like himself

>>he does not go into the interior
>>he engages in dangerous local currency
>>exchanges
>>runs into danger of being killed, or expelled
>>by local authorities

>>he contacts higher authority of country 'behind'
>>>the local authority
>>they let him stay on
>>>then he leaves

he frequents burial grounds in these non-Western countries
his imagination is dominated by images

of tunnels	being buried
potholes	being buried alive
dunes	

? issues connected with implantation

One can stop, in a certain sense at any stage
One can lose one's *continuity* at any stage
Then one's cut-off past is liable to keep on replaying itself,
even taking over the life cycle.

Many people feel they have never been born
Others feel they have never been implanted
Others are *just* implanted, unreconciled, pining, mourning,
crying for the moon, the ghost of themselves as blastula
before burial in the womb.

'The life of the individual repeats the life of the
species.' So in the womb the embryo passes through the
image states of tens of thousands of antecedent years of its
development. In this state it is not unreasonable to suppose that
the developing foetus may be at best somewhat subject to the
images of the mother, who may be trying desperately to get rid
of it. Her communications to the sensitive image of the foetus
must surely be somehow different from those of the mother who
is welcoming the new life, with its developing image enshrined
in her heart.*

And I would not rule out the possibility that the
embryo may communicate to the mother.

*E. Graham Howe, *Cure or Heal*, Allen and Unwin, London,
1965, p. 110.

She had a miscarriage two hours after awakening from this
dream.

> she is wandering through Jerusalem
> all is in ruins and crumbling
> there is nothing to grip
> no house to enter

She wonders whether this may have been the dream of the
embryo.

A dream of the night before a miscarriage in the morning,
several hours later.

> She is in a sealed car at the centre of a cross-
> roads at dead of night. The traffic lights are not
> working: cars travelling back and forth, up and
> down, whizz by. She is in terror. She frantically
> tries to get out but can't.

This woman was convinced the dream was the embryo's.

Woman   she wanted to get out and got out.
             I don't blame her
Me   how do you know it was a her
Woman   I just know it

> During the night (two months pregnant) she woke
herself, several times, crying out in her sleep, 'I must get out.
I want out. Let me out.'
> In the morning, she had a spontaneous abortion,
against all conscious intention.

The following is a commonplace event to psychiatrists.

> a young person
> takes to his/her room
> discards his/her clothes

huddles up in what is commonly called a
'foetal position',
or adopts another position
which he/she may stay in for hours,
even days on end,
urinates and defecates without moving
the person loses interest in talking or
being spoken to
he gives indications of great disturbance if
'interrupted' by external stimuli

This type of behaviour almost irresistibly reminds
those who see it
of the unclothed foetus in a womb.

The person concerned will often openly say that
that is how he or she feels.

It is not uncommon nowadays for me to hear
people tell of their birth or of their uterine life, as memories
of their own, which they have never forgotten, or forgotten
and remembered 'spontaneously', in the course of psychotherapy, a 'freak out', a psychedelic episode, or some form
of primal or radical therapy.
Thousands of people in every walk of life, of both
sexes, in all income groups, of all ages, claim to remember
their birth and before,
or to go through experiences, which seem to
them to be *re*-experiences of, and transforms of,
natal and prenatal experiences.
For a long time, I was put off these stories,
somewhat, by my sense of their antecedent improbability.
But?

Let me restate the argument of the past few pages.
I have to report that many of my contemporaries
feel that what has happened from their conception to and
through birth has a relevance of some kind or other to them

now as adults. These feeling patterns deserve serious attention. It does not seem to me to be, *a priori*, nonsense, or antecedently impossible, that prenatal patterns may be mapped onto natal and postnatal experience.

A stockbroker, aged forty

from time to time very
intensely, at other times
always, but less so he feels
exposed,
naked
raw
flayed   stripped of vernix caseosa
helpless
at the mercy of others
no strength
it feels to him
as if he were a newborn baby
he has devised a procedure
that mitigates his torment
he covers himself
or has his wife cover him   restoration of foetal or
in leather   newborn skin feeling
covered in leather he feels   as yet unborn
as though he is mummified
and has oil poured
between his skin and leather
affording him one of the most
pleasant and consoling
'feelings' – sensations he
knows

I am not considering whether these analogues are 'right', if that is a sensible issue, but merely that they are actual. All of them I have heard or read, as well as made myself, before or after having heard or read them.

May there be a placental–umbilical–uterine stage
of development preceding the breast–oral stage?

Could some babies be confused by the
disappearance of the cord and placenta?

Could cord and placenta
sometimes take on phantom limb–like
phenomena in infancy and later life?

I am impressed by the fact that 'I' was once
placenta, umbilical cord, and foetus.
Many people seem to confuse the placenta with
the uterus. The placenta, amniotic sack, umbilical cord (all the
foetal 'membranes') are cellularily, biologically, physically,
genetically, *me*. All of *me* I left behind in the womb,
or was cut off from forever when my umbilical cord was
cut.
It seems to me more than likely that many of us
are suffering lasting effects from our umbilical cords being
cut too soon.
Is it necessary to cut them at all?
If one waits, it withers away 'of its own accord'.
What's the harm in waiting? It has been suggested that we may
lose 30 per cent of the blood we would have if our cord and
placenta, together with the circulatory system connected with
them in us, were allowed to phase itself out naturally. Since it
does do so *naturally*, why interfere with the natural course of
events?
If all is going well, there seems to be no risk
involved to the life of mother or child in *not* clamping and
cutting the cord, at least before it has stopped pulsating.
Under such happy circumstances, not cutting the
cord does not seem in the least to affect adversely the onset of
breathing. In fact I suspect that usually, in normal circumstances, breathing and the rhythm of the heart are greatly
disturbed, perhaps for life, by clamping (throttling) the
umbilical cord and then cutting it, while it and the placenta are
still fully functionally *us*
comparable to the guillotine?
strangulation?

the steady throb, the quiet beat
still echoes in the pulse of feet

scratch the wind
try being kind

too late too late
one can but hate

the two way flow
's no where to go

such perturbation
brings on transcendental meditation

that cringe
craves the syringe

Could we be haunted by our placenta
    our intra-uterine

          twin
          lover
          rival
          double?

Could the placenta
be the original
life giver
life sucker

our first friend or our first persecutor
tormentor?*

* Many of the above suggestions, and more, have been put forward by Francis J. Mott in an extensive series of articles and monographs from the early thirties to the present. This, as yet, largely neglected corpus requires a separate study. I mention here only one of his books, wherein he himself gives a condensed summary of some of his work: *The Nature of the Self,* The Integration Publishing Co., London and New York, 1959.

the analogy between

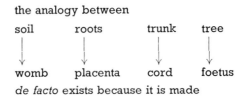

soil	roots	trunk	tree
womb	placenta	cord	foetus

de facto exists because it is made

My daughter aged two and a half says to new
au pair girl

'Are you a Brenda?'
Brenda was the first au pair girl

It is as though
we say to the breast
are you a placenta?
to a relationship one is about to get *into*
are you a good womb?

the first of the series becomes the category name
of the series

foetus   cord   placenta in womb
              umbilical   umbilical
              arteries   vein

    Adam   tree   Eve   in garden
                  and serpent
      fruit   tree   roots   soil
                  trunk
                  two–way flow
                  give and take

St George   spear   dragon
                                                  cave
                                         maiden

              two snakes   staff
                  triple structure
                  caduceus

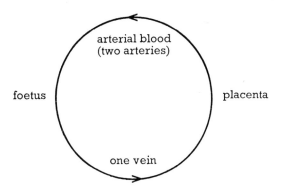

{ place of exertion
{ source of food

is it possible that the *anlage* of these patterns may begin to be registered by our organism before we are born?

placenta –
             my other self
             my twin, sister, brother
             my incestuous lover
             my not-me me
                 the pre-transitional object

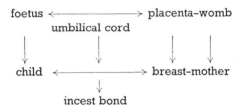

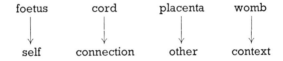

Grief for the Placenta and Cord

When I was eight I went one late winter afternoon with both my parents to see *Lost Horizon* with Ronald Colman.

When I came home, I ate a bowl of porridge.

The taste of the porridge seemed to merge with the death of the Princess from Shangri-La in the blizzard and snow as they are making their way across the mountains and the image of the young princess, ageing decades in seconds, crumbling, dissolving into a wizened old hag, and finally to dust.

Both felt closely akin to a very early 'impression', before words, before images.

Shangri-La   princess turns to old woman
    | and crumbles to dust
    ↓   ↓
womb   placenta withers and dies

One could remain in love with one's placenta the rest of one's life.

Could I have registered the ageing and dying of my intra-uterine lover, and could that impress have been reverberated by a configurational resonance?

6   Birth

To be born is a momentous event in our life
cycle. In recent years hundreds of thousands of people have
been going through experiences as adults which they themselves feel to be related to their actual birth experience.
Traces of the experience of being born seem to occur in
dreams, myths, fantasies, physical events, or to be acted out
in different ways.

The preference for unnatural childbirth practices,
which seems to be spreading across the world, despite
countermovements to tune into the natural process, has led
birth, in many places, to be a major psychobiological disaster
zone, in which almost everything is done the exact opposite
way from how it would happen, if allowed to.

This is properly the subject of a separate book.*

She is twenty-six

she sits on the floor hunched
holding a cigarette in each hand
puffing in and out smoke from both through her mouth

* Frederick Leboyer, *Birth Without Violence*, Alfred A. Knopf,
New York, 1975; Doris Haire, 'The Cultural Warping of Childbirth', *Inter-*
national Childbirth Education Association, vol. II, no. 1.

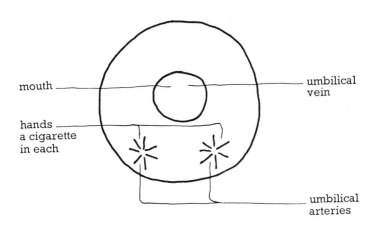

a terror takes
over my whole body
a sense of *doom*
it feels like I'm going
to be chucked out
of the country
that my world
is going
to collapse
I'm going to be suffocated

then, she is
reduced to state of complete
helplessness
terror
her world feels it does collapse
she is scattered
lost
no energy
almost dead
can just lie in bed and sleep

projection into
the future
of
memory
from
past
viz., just before
uterine contractions

how it felt
just after birth

everything is all right, then
the world
it's going to kill me
crush me again and again
the terror is eating at me
it's like
being born = being minced
                = being eaten
                = being *munched* in a mouth
uterus   = mouth
uterine contractions feel like being munched in a mouth

The Compression Syndrome

the world is crushing me
the world is falling in on me
I am crib'd, cabined, confined,
I have no room
no room to manoeuvre
no room to turn
I am suffocated
I am stifled
I am smothered
there is pressure from all sides,
                        from all directions

it's a process of building up dreams,
constructing a world,
then BAM
it's all taken away
and I'm afraid I set it up that way for myself
I could provoke you or something, anything
just to flair up and kill me
so that I bring about my own destruction

                            world collapse
                            my own destruction
my own birth   crushed
                            chucked out

I gave the signal for my own birth

uterine contractions ⟶ terror

terror bears the *impress* of the
uterine contractions
so that terror itself is
becomes, as it were, the uterine contractions

present	past
I	foetus
live in	lived in a
terror	womb of terror
things seem to be all right	just before birth

it starts to crush me
again and again
I know I cannot stand
any more of it
I am completely helpless
and exhausted and
I lose all my money = blood
I just want to lie in bed curled
up, naked, under blankets be
tube fed : not even bottle fed

so *terror* now *behaves* like uterine contractions

uterine contractions persist as terror contractions

uterine contractions
being beaten   being chewed
being flayed alive   being minced
being crucified
being ground down

11 Nov. 1972 New York

After giving talk at Hunter College Auditorium,
went to a commune on 10th St, which was centred around
a small, frail, chain-smoking lady in her fifties.

She had been a psychotherapist for twelve years.

One day a man of twenty-four was in her office. He had run
away from a mental hospital where he had been told (after his
third suicide attempt) that he was an incurable psychotic, and
if he did not have a lobotomy, he would have to be com-
mitted for the rest of his life, probably.

He had felt (he told me) all his life, stuck, as it were, in a
manhole; he could not get in or out.

In her office two years ago he began to go into writhing,
twisting movements (catatonic stereotyped movements
supposedly).

It occurred to her that he was trying to be born.

He slithered from his chair to the floor,
and she enacted with him his birth, playing the part of the
midwife. It was over in about twenty minutes. He was delivered.

> He was out of the manhole, he felt,
> for the first time in his life.
> He felt completely different.
> No longer desperate, or frantic.

Subsequently he went through other 'birthings'.
> Now he has a girlfriend. Is working. Looks,
> moves, talks ordinarily.

He was the first. Now, Elizabeth had 'birthed' over a hundred
people, both sexes, all ages; some, many times.

That evening, in front of forty to fifty people, in the presence
of a camera team
> she 'birthed' seven people.

One of the cameramen had a go. I went through. A nineteen-
year-old girl who was a Yoga teacher went through it; a fifty-
four-year-old scholar.

One girl of sixteen had been diagnosed psychotic.
She looked listless, eyes lustreless, skin flat, dry.
She writhed, squirmed, contracted, agonized on the floor for
about fifteen minutes until she felt she 'came out'.

The change in fifteen minutes was remarkable.

Her eyes were bright, almost glistening. Her skin
warm and moist. She said she realized, with
wonder, a feeling she could not remember ever
having before.

She had always felt touched,
        but, until now, had never experienced *touching*
– and had never realized until the sensation of *touching* arose,
that it had been missing. Consequently, she said, she had
always felt both fearful of contact, and a need to cling.
Now, suddenly, this was gone.
        I heard, two years later, she was still 'all right'.

This lady midwife came over to London in 1973, and spent a
fortnight doing 'birthing' sessions, with people in the house-
holds and network in our scene in London. Many of them very
disturbed; psychiatrists, therapists, patients. The most remarkable changes came over people in fifteen to twenty minutes. I
saw her go through over twenty birthings one afternoon and
evening.
        Subsequently, we have developed 'birthing' as
one of the components of our practice in London.*

        I have told this story since in more detail to many
psychiatrists, throughout the world.

        What about the transference? What about
        suggestion? Merely symptomatic, surely, etc.

No one ever asked me how to get in touch with her.
She is now dead.

* For details of Elizabeth Fehr's technique: Leslie Feher, The
Elizabeth Fehr Natal Therapy Institute, 3 East 80th Street, Floor B, New York, New
York 10021.

7   Cutting the Umbilical Cord

White American woman, aged twenty-six, talking of her birth:

> 'I was a breech; but they turned me upside down,
> then dragged me out with forceps – I still feel the
> pain coming up on the right side . . .
> . . . eventually I came out. I had had a helluva
> time of it, but could still actually smile.
> Then they cut the cord.
> That's when I knew the fuckers really meant
> business.'

the insult to injury

When the cord is cut immediately after birth, the instant the cord is cut (between the two places it has just been tied), there may be a jerk of the *whole* baby, including fingers and toes.

I have seen a global organismic reaction occur the instant the cord is cut. It would appear to be neurologically impossible. There are no nerves in the umbilical cord. But it *does* happen. I've *seen* it happen. It does not always happen however.

Therefore there is transmission of a very fast and global order mediated somehow from the site of the cut, through the cord, transmitted, it seems, *to* neural tissue from non-neural tissue.

This presumably must happen somehow. How it does happen is totally unknown. However the fact that it *does* happen settles the question about whether it *can* happen.

The issue as to whether it *does* happen can be settled very soon by direct observation, on those babies born in good enough shape to be reacting in a healthy way. This observation alone impels us to admit that there must be a domain of ignorance stretching further than we can peer.

	The response to 'What may it have been like then?' reveals at least
(i)	one's *present* projections onto our *past*, and may give an indication of
(ii)	how we did experience the past.

How we now feel about a past that is beyond conscious recall does not necessarily tell us anything about the *past* as it was then. It may only tell of our present reactions, of our present responses, of our present fantasies of then.

A woman says that she is now convinced that the high temperature and feeling of being desperately ill and going to die at a certain time of the year, always called the 'flu', is some physical memory of living through some intrauterine crisis when she was about three months old. For her 'flu' always comes on three months after her conception date.

Many people in the course of their therapy nowadays go through 'numbers' which feel to them, spontaneously, like again going over prenatal experiences, all the way back to conception. Some people go back to past lifetimes.

I have looked through a few textbooks on obstetrics and pediatrics, to find any reference to what it may feel like to be born,

and to encounter the outside world for the first time in the first seconds, minutes, hours, days and weeks.

Not the slightest suggestion anywhere that the
creature being brought into our world from his or her world
heretofore is one of us, a few years younger,
        who is,
        I would say *obviously*
        if you look at him or her (that is, not zonked, etc.)
        an exquisitely sentient being
        seeming to be reacting all over
        to everything.
        I would say that the baby at birth is *feeling* it.

        Thousands of adults now say they can remember
feeling it, and remember it in their feelings.

        If we have indeed here an exquisitely alive and
sentient being, like ourselves, even perhaps in a sense
more so,

                might we not consider it logical
                that we would do our best to
                arrange the first extra-uterine environment
                into which
                we bring a newcomer,
                in such a way
                that would be most natural
                                most safe
                most welcoming
                most soft, gentle, tender, loving, human,
                non-disruptive
                harmonious,
                pleasant to the sense of sight
                pleasant to the sense of hearing
                pleasant to the sense of smell
                pleasant to the sense of taste
pleasant to our sense of pulse, posture, movement, timing
instead of the isometric opposites of these common-sense
desiderata in many of the most technologically
advanced obstetric centres?

The way the whole birth process is shredded to pieces by technological interference is a most remarkable feature of our time.

A man in his thirties went back to his homeland after some years. Going back, he felt more open, as though his navel was open and very vulnerable.

As he crosses the border *from* his homeland, away again, he feels a hardening, a knotting, a tightening and closing up again around the navel, and inside the navel.

what was once momentous
may shrivel to an apparently trivial memento

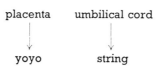

placenta   umbilical cord

yoyo   string

Woman   He said he wanted a divorce
            I had not expected it
            It was a body blow
            right here (pointing to navel)

After a lecture I gave on some aspects of birth, including cutting the cord, a young doctor said to me, with considerable intensity and urgency:

Doctor   but we have to break the flow
Me   but why?
Doctor   (stopped dead in his tracks, as it were – pause)
            Right. Right.
            but why do we do it then?
Me   it's just occurred to you for the first time,
            about five seconds ago . . .
            it's a very good question for us to ponder for
            some time

8   Self–Description

The surgeon's hands cannot afford to tremble with compassion. The nurse's eyes must be dry. But if we are *au fait* with our feelings, we may restrain them at one time, and let them be unrestrained at others.

The more aware of our feelings, the more competent we are likely to be in restraining them when necessary, and the more easily will we loosen such restraint when circumstances no longer seem to require it.

Also in this way we will not need to use up any more energy than necessary.

The release of pent-up feelings almost always seems to be refreshing and energizing, so long as they do not explode into destructive conduct which we later have good reason to regret.

When I remember an incident in my life, I can recall it in two ways, from 'inside' or 'outside', as it were.

e.g. aged four

I am standing behind a closed door listening to my parents talking in the other room.

I can remember that situation from how I felt in it.

Or I can *see* myself standing behind the door.

As far as I remember, I did not *see* myself from the outside at the time.

There are many records of people who see themselves, or seem to see themselves, from outside themselves.

These are varieties of 'out-of-the-body' experiences, which seem to me to be more common than many people suppose. How common no one knows.

It seems to come naturally to us to represent in a visualizable formula events we *feel*, but do not see, and cannot *see*.

If we want to *show* how we *feel*, we may, for instance if we *feel twisted*, represent this nonvisual pattern of feeling by a visual pattern of movement, or design.

The feeling of being central, of being *here*, may be represented by a dot we can see out *there*.

The first time I ever got completely pissed was in Crianlarach, on a Saturday night during a weekend in the hills, with the Glasgow University Mountaineering Club, as a first-year medical student.

I had imbibed quantities of rum, gin, whisky, beer, and Guinness, and was now lying face down on a country road, about 11.00 pm in slush, snow, vomit, all under the stars.

Too far gone to turn over, or get up.

The world is turning. I am suspended from it. I ineffectually try to move my fingers with a view to clutching the ground, to prevent myself falling off.

Useless. I'm past it. When I shut my eyes I could be anywhere. In fact there is no 'I' to be found. Just whirling scattered elements.

Very very unpleasant; and strangely unstrange. Could I have felt that way before?

I had been resting my mind in a quiet place for days. Only consciousness and space as one. No I. No awareness of any object. The thought of a thought occurred. That very mere wisp, which ordinarily would have felt lighter than a piece of fluff, weighed an enormous weight, like a Magritte rock in the sky.

It was so heavy and an 'I' that had not been there before already was feeling heavy itself . . .

Did I weigh any more on the scales?

A consciousness can exist with or without a sense of an ego, an identity.

We are clear that the ego is a mental construction intimately chemically conditioned. It can dissolve completely, between two seconds of nitrous oxide, or any quick-acting ego-dissolving drug.

Changes in the chemical environment of our brains change our minds.

Should people be allowed free access to the chemical controls of their minds?

Or should these chemical switches be under very stringent governmental controls throughout the world?

This is one of the very few matters where all governments seem to see more or less eye to eye.

At 17.15 almost every day for several years,
I feel like a drink (of wine, of whisky, of vodka)

Sometimes I restrain myself
Sometimes I let myself have it

Why do I want it then?

I often know *when* it is 17.15 by the feeling that comes over me

Why?

Has it anything to do with the hour of my birth, 17.15?

Or with my *idea* of the hour of my birth?

A late afternoon in February 1965

I am weary. Exhausted and dispirited. Fifteen years of study and research into 'wisdom, madness, and folly' have left me, it seems, none the wiser. Vanity of vanities.

I lay myself out on the floor of my consulting room at 21 Wimpole Street, stretched out on my back in the 'death' asana.

I shut my eyes. Drift off. As I do, I ask, with all my heart, if there is a power of healing, to give me some indication of its nature.

I am in a pleasant English country house. Large room, French windows. It is a gentle late summer afternoon. An older man, perhaps in his sixties, enters the room. He looks rather like one of those English scholars, who maybe once was a colonel, or something like that.

We have never met before but he does not seem a stranger. He suggests we go for a walk.

As we are walking, I become aware of the sun. It seems to draw nearer: to become larger and hotter. It becomes an all-encompassing fiery furnace. Until I am absorbed in and by it completely, reduced to one cinder.

I have returned to that dot again. Bindu? I am aware I can go beyond it. If I do, it could mean physical death. I am between life and death.

I find myself lying on the floor of my consulting room. I cannot move. I cannot lift my eyelids. I cannot move my eyeballs. I cannot lift a finger. Breathing is happening. I can hear the throb of my heart and blood.

I want to move now. I scan around my body to see if I can move anything. Eventually a muscle in my right cheek twitches. I feel a 'line'; very thin energy channel running down right side of face. I can just twang it; then the side of my mouth; then my tongue; then my right thumb; then I can open my eyes, and now I can roll over on the floor. I'm out of it. Back again.

I am back.   Time: about thirty minutes

I remember that one cinder, that dot, that point.* When I was three I heard my father say to my mother: 'I'm going to beat him to an inch of his life this time.'

I knew I was in for it.

---

* 'The natural soul of man is not larger than a single point; and upon these points the shape and character of the whole heaven, be it a hundred times as large as it is, is imprinted *potentialialer*.' Johann Kepler, quoted in W. Pauli, op. cit., p. 182.

> He beat me. As he did, he began 'literally' to
> smash me to pieces.

> I knew there was nothing more to be done.
> I contracted to a point.
> There no one could get me.
> On the other side of that point was . . . where I
> came from?

> After a while, I ventured out again.
> The coast was clear. The damage was not
> irreparable.

Cut-ups and Cut-offs

I awake and remember a dream. I remember that during the dream 'I' was 'in' the dream. I even believe I dreamt the dream. I, awake, do not feel quite the same as (i) the dreamer of the dream, or (ii) the I in the dream, as a dramatis persona. I am now the rememberer and forgetter of the dreamed dream, the dreamed I. How have these cut-ups and cut-offs of me come about? How can it even be described?

In awakening there seem to be rapid positional shifts between

(i) I^1 who dreamt (actively) the dream (its author, choreographer, etc.)

(ii) I^2 who dreamt (passively) the dream (its audience)

(iii) I^3 who acted a part in the dream (actor)

(iv)   waking I^1 perhaps remembers a little or nothing of a dream, perhaps nothing of I^1, I^2, I^3.

However, from a theoretical position that I^1 may adopt, I^1, I^2, I^3, I^4, are all chips off the same block. And from a consciousness I^0, antecedent to I^1, I^2, I^3, and I^4, I^0, I^2, I^3 . . . I^{n+1} are regarded as One. But am I single or multiple? Am I, indeed, at all? From my interrogation of my own experience I receive no unequivocal answer.

What happens whereby I^1 has lost its experiential connection with I^3, I^2, I^1, and I^0?

There may be cut-off points: these could be between I^0 and I^1, I^1 and I^2, I^2 and I^3, etc.

1969. About 8.00 pm after a long tiring day in my office on
Wimpole Street, walk out into London, December. Turn right.
Turn left. Turn right. Health Food Shop on Baker Street. Jar of
honey. Hail a taxi. Home.

From Wimpole Street to Health Food Shop on
Baker Street is a walk of twenty minutes I would not have
made, if I had not wanted a taste of honey.

A taste of honey was worth more to me than
twenty minutes with Jutta and our child.

Moreover,

all of the millions of cells of me were moved,
without 'conscious' awareness of endorsement, twenty
minutes and one quarter of a mile besides where I thought I
wanted to go . . .

Is not this a serious state of affairs?

I am sitting in my chair, in my consulting room, listening to
someone, in the late afternoon.

I reach out with my left hand for a glass of water
beside me.

As I lay my hand on the glass, I pause, and ask
myself:

Why am I about to sip some water at this
moment?

I'm not thirsty

I'm not dehydrated

Did I just hear something that gave a twinge I
didn't notice and . . .

no I don't think so

I feel relaxed

My mouth?

the taste in it is hardly noticeable,

It's not objectionable, now I focus on it

But my mouth is dry.

Strange it takes me so long to work out that,
ostensibly at least, I seem to want to drink 'because' my
mouth is dry.

Why is it dry?

I don't know why it's dry. There's nothing wrong as far as I know with my salivary glands.

I try to salivate deliberately, without drinking, at will.

I can. To my surprise it is easy.

My mouth is now pleasantly moist.

I no longer want that drink.

A party at a friend's house.

He has invited several Indian musicians.

We sit on the floor, crowded, and begin to compose ourselves to listen, as they start to tune up.

There is a large dog on the floor near me.

As everyone becomes quiet, and as the music begins, stuff from the dog seems to be irritating my nasal passages. I have always had an allergic diathesis. I am in more and more difficulties, trying to stop sneezing. I desperately try to stop sneezing but it is useless. As the music begins to get under way, I have to get up and out, picking my way through, between, over, across fifty people densely packed on the floor.

Excuse me, excuse sorry ex- (sneeze) -cuse me sorry, etc., until out.

The dog and I had been close together in the room before the music began.

I didn't start to sneeze until the music began to get under way, and I realized it was not very good. In fact not good enough (for me) to sit there through it without squirming and cringing.

The sneezing got me out of it. But I delayed seeing this entirely clearly until it had served its purpose. I could blame it on a 'thing' I had, or something from the dog.

Only when I got out, I 'realized', I 'admitted' to myself, I had not been sneezing 'at' the dog, but 'at' the music.

I am sitting in my room. A young man is sitting facing me
I am filling my pipe

I begin to feel he is impatiently waiting for me to finish
I look at him. Actually he does not look impatient with me. He
        seems very much absorbed in his own misery
        I look at my feeling that he is impatient

        The feeling, as I look at it, opens out to a memory
of me aged fifteen sitting in a chair, feeling impatient, and
feeling ashamed of feeling impatient, watching my grannie
(my mother's mother, over eighty) getting a meal ready for
me, after school, my mother having gone to the hospital for
an operation.

        Thirty-two years ago,
        I was feeling impatient with my grannie
        now
        I feel he feels impatient with me
        she was preparing food for me
        I feel he feels I am preparing food for him
        a clear example of a mild transient
        'counter-transference' projection
        I attribute to him now, toward me,
        feelings I had had then toward grannie

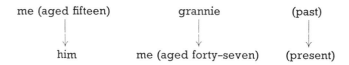

me (aged fifteen)   grannie   (past)

        him   me (aged forty-seven)   (present)

        As my awareness of the above opens out
        my feeling that he is impatient with me fades
        into feeling impatient with him, briefly, and this
        feeling in turn turns into a feeling of impatience
        with myself, again briefly (a few seconds), to
        then fade out completely.

I am lying in the sun doing nothing.
I notice I am breathing in and out of my right nostril.
        When I try to breathe in or out of my left nostril
I am thwarted. It seems totally blocked. Is it blocked by a

mechanical obstruction? If so, it must have arisen very quickly, within twenty-four hours, because I'm as sure as anything I was breathing freely through it at least as late as yesterday.

Are the air passages congested on the left side? but not on the right? The right side is completely free. I have no 'cold'. I am not aware of catarrh, or an allergic sinusitis, confined to the left side.

It is puzzling. It engages my attention. I become impatient and angry with whatever is going on. I try to push the breath out as hard as I can. I'm afraid I'll burst a blood vessel. I try as hard again to pull it in. To no avail.

I decide to pinpoint my mind. Let everything go, and then see what has happened. I do so. While my egoic consciousness is in abeyance, the left nostril begins to let air through perfectly freely. I revert to my usual egoic consciousness. After a few seconds it is blocked again.

I repeat the observation at least three times.
1) In a non-egoic pinpointed consciousness it is open.
2) In my egoic consciousness it is blocked.
The correlation seems clearly observed. But how is this effect being achieved?

The mental/physical operations subtending this trick are beyond the ken of my scrutiny. Unbeknown.

Why? And even, is why a proper question? intelligent question?

I've got a glimpse of what is happening. I don't know *how*, and I don't know *why*.

I start to talk to Jutta about my father, an old man, who has lost most of his memory, and is unlikely to live much longer.

> I start to fumble with my hands, with my words, there is a welling up all through my body . . .
> a 'rush' of . . .
> I suddenly become more acutely aware of everything.

I look away from her. I fix my eyes on a pattern on the floor to my right. It begins to go out of focus: my eyes fill with tears, they well up, run over, run down my face. My

nose and sinuses become congested: shining clear fluid,
thicker than tears, pours abundantly out of both nostrils and
runs down my face.

I can't breathe through my nose.

An urgent ache appears in the back of my throat.
All my respiratory system is being tossed around like a small
boat in a very stormy sea.

My diaphragm, intercostal muscles, abdominal
muscles, my tongue and facial muscles are heaving incoher-
ently. If I try to control their juncture it will probably induce
an attack of asthma. If I let it rip –

My face completely dissolves (when it used to be
more brittle than it is now, I would have said it 'cracked up').

Fibrillations in both cheeks.
Involuntary retraction of the lips

> sobbing, and moaning,
> unrestrained
> for two or three minutes
> then over.

This sort of behaviour remains a mystery to me
> incoherence
> speechlessness
> change of consciousness
> unusual physical feelings
> widespread disturbances of physiological
> function
> involving a global reaction through all sectors of
> the CNS
> endocrine, muscular systems, etc.
> changes in respiratory
> and cardiovascular systems

9   Samples of Psychiatry

> If fire is lighted in water
> How is it to be extinguished?
>
> If the fear comes from the protector
> Who is there to protect you from this fear?
>
> Nagarjuna, *The Tree of Wisdom*, verse 79*

The first psychiatric 'clinical demonstration' I attended was in my fourth year as a medical student.

It was in a small amphitheatre in the Glasgow Western Infirmary. About two dozen medical students, including three or four female students, sat on the tiered benches and below us the consultant 'interviewed' several patients, all 'out' patients.

He asked them each their name, age, address, the composition of their families, had they any previous illnesses, and then inquired after their present complaint.

The first patient that afternoon was a thin, pale, bespectacled chap of seventeen, with marked acne. He had been referred to the psychiatric department by his general practitioner, to whom he had gone for treatment of his acne. But the GP believed in 'psychosomatic' medicine, which psychiatrists knew more about.

The consultant and patient had not met before.

After two minutes during which he answered correctly the questions asked (all this information was already in a letter from his doctor; the point of the questions was not

* Translated by Major W. L. Campbell, C.I.E., Baptist Mission Press, Calcutta, 1919.

to provide us with the facts of life, age, etc., but to establish
whether he was 'correctly orientated for time, place, and
person' or not).

Consultant	and what is your complaint, apart from your acne, which we can all see?
Patient	I'm afraid people are looking at me in the street
Consultant	you are afraid they know you masturbate
Patient	(His white face turned scarlet, and his red pimples went white)
	yes
Consultant	how often do you masturbate?
Patient	two or three times a week

And so the interview went on for about fifteen
minutes (longer than usual).

The patient was then dismissed, and a discussion
ensued on this case for about five minutes before the next one
was brought in.

I had never heard the word 'masturbate' used
'in public' before.

I cringed in terror at the prospect of the consultant asking us the questions he asked this patient, but he did
not. He explained that masturbation used to be regarded as a
cause of mental deterioration, but more advanced medical
opinion now thought of it as not usually 'an etiological factor',
but merely an early symptom of some conditions. He pointed
out that the patient had answered all his questions dispassion-
ately without a tremor in his face, and apart from the vascular
changes in his facial blood vessels, no changes occurred in
his outward behaviour.

In all but exceptional cases 'psychotherapy' was
contraindicated as making patients 'worse'. There might be a
'spontaneous remission', or an 'arrest' in the 'process', or . . .

Dr MacKenzie at Stobhill had a way with
involuntial melancholics.

When one of these Lowlands Presbyterian sixty-
year-olds came in lamenting his certain and justly preordained
damnation for his unredeemable deadly sins, with wringing of

hands, groaning, loss of appetite, engrossed in self-loathing at his own self-pity, constipated, having been brought into the hospital finally because no one could put up with him any longer, insufferable, his remedy was 10cc of turpentine injection into the buttocks. This produced a raging fever, hopefully sterile (sterile pyrexia), and swollen burning buttocks, exquisitely painful.

'We'll give him a taste of what he thinks is coming to him (hell fire as adumbrated by fever, torture by the wracking pain, the delirium, etc.) and we'll see, when it dies down (after ten days), if he is not going to shut up and count his blessings.'

Nobody had been heard to come back for more.

100 per cent remission rate. 100 per cent discharge rate. 0 per cent relapse rate.

Clinical Conference

She is in the hospital because every time her husband, a travelling salesman, comes home she starts to vomit and continues to do so until he leaves.

She denies being sick of him

Is she *really* sick of him,
          can't admit it to herself
                    denies the thought,
          but converted to a physical metaphor
                    it expresses itself as
                    an hysterical conversion symptom?

(genital sexual difficulties and early oral problems, no doubt)

perhaps she is vomiting
                    out umbilical blood via her mouth
                    confusing him with her placenta?
perhaps she wants to vomit over him
                    as revenge for his going away?

perhaps she wants to get her bad indigestible feelings out of
       her system. Which in a way she does by 'converting'
       feelings to stomach contents, then getting rid of them
       by vomiting?
perhaps it is some transform of a . . . ?
perhaps it's some ectohormonal mismatch?
perhaps a birth trauma?
perhaps psychotherapy?
perhaps tranquillizers?
perhaps behaviour therapy?
perhaps an interview with the husband?
perhaps marital therapy?
perhaps a home visit by a social worker?
perhaps a physical examination of the woman by a physician?
perhaps testing by clinical psychologist?
perhaps group psychotherapy?

She gets very depressed before she starts vomiting
right   or before he comes home
right
right   well how about a few bangs with the box before he
comes home or before she starts vomiting, it might break the
coupling and the periodicity . . .
maybe   we'll think about it

Case Conference

Early 1970s, East Coast of USA

     Man of 24: catatonic schizophrenic about to be
discharged, remitted after eight months, electric shocks,
tranquillizers, psychotherapy

Patient (to me)	when I came back from Vietnam, it was too confusing. Too complex. I had to try to figure it out. I had to get rid of all the lumber. So I finally made no movements at all. They carted me here. And started doing me in. I realized that I couldn't simplify my life this way, so I started to move normally again, and talk

normally, so they've reduced the tranquillizers
and stopped the electric shocks and I believe
they are going to let me leave shortly

Patient's   but John I thought you were really cured and
Psycho-   now I hear you have just been putting on a show
therapist   to get out. John, I am disappointed in you.

Early 1970s, UK

father and mother
two daughters
              one thirteen
              the other twelve Anne
the younger one is the problem
              she is always running away from home
              she does not apply herself to her schoolwork
              she is untidy
              she is sloppy
in fact her mother can't bear even to look at her
              she did not want another baby so soon after the
              first
              she wanted a boy, if it had to be something

              since she had Anne
              she has become fat,
              lost her looks,
              her husband no longer finds her attractive
              she hates her
              and resents her
              she often beats her up
              Anne cannot do a thing right

Anne is in psychotherapy? Schizophrenic

              there seems nothing the matter with Anne
              she runs away because her mother whips her
              her mother whips her for running away

              will her mother have her revenge
              by driving her crazy

or is it possible
that her mother might *repent* and *relent*?

forgive,
and possibly be forgiven

forgive us our trespasses,
as we forgive them their trespass against us

He is twenty four. He has been having an electroshock every three weeks because
      the effect of the electric shock wears off after ten
days and then
      he keeps going into deep thought
      to do this he has to go into a room
      he must not be interrupted
      he has to concentrate with a total effort
      he cannot afford to complicate matters
      by making a single movement
      by uttering a single word
      he stays awake as much as possible because the
process is interrupted by sleep
      he is uninterested in eating
      he takes off his clothes
      he pisses and shits where he is standing, or
sitting, or lying, immobile

      as he gets deeper
      he feels he gets closer
      tremendous pressure begins to come upon him
from all around
      it is like being born, he says

      every time it is stopped, compulsively, by
electric shocks
      he has to start from the beginning again

      There is not *one* psychiatric installation known to
me in the UK, and perhaps two or three in the USA where he
would be 'allowed', or even 'helped', to go 'through' what
he feels impelled to go into.

There is no place known to me where a young
or old psychiatrist may, as a matter of pure research interest,
be allowed to observe the natural history of this process,

could he be trying to go through a birth
experience?

Is it possible that in an appropriate environment,
and with skilled therapists as accoucheurs, he might be
'delivered'?

Could his actual 'symptoms', if one could be on
the 'right' side of them, be the channel through which he
might find release from his agony?

As it is,

he says he will kill himself if he is not allowed
to go 'into' his deep thoughts,

a further indication for more electric shocks
Moreover, the psychiatrists now feel he has become 'addicted'
to electric shocks,

since he keeps on forcing them to administer
them and some ways and means have to be found to 'wean'
him off them. Perhaps brain surgery before it is too late.

A little bit of his brain cut off from the rest now
may save more having to be cut off later.

A psychiatrist regrets to me that there had not
been ECT at the time of Shakespeare, for then *King Lear* would
never have needed to have been written; he would have had
ECT.

A frantic looking woman asked: 'If I do not feel
I exist, why should I not kill myself?'

'A trivial philosophical question,' replied the
chairman of her department of philosophy.

Case Conference

They met in Austria, her home. Moved to Aust-
ralia, where neither had ever been. Then he was sent to
South America. And now they live somewhere in Northeastern
America.

He is away all day
She knows no one

One day when he comes home she tells him she
feels like screaming. He phones the doctor. He gives her
an injection. He calls an ambulance. She is taken to a sana-
torium. She feels like screaming. She is put on a régime of
tranquillizers – she feels even more like screaming – and
electric shocks. She starts to feel like screaming again after
the immediate concussion of electric shocks wears off.

She is put on psychotherapy. Electric shocks
discontinued, tranquillizers retained and reduced, plus a few
other things.

She came in three months ago
She is still in
She still feels like screaming
She has never screamed

Chicago, 1972

Her father is a hefty construction worker
Her mother is made to the same proportions
Her two big brothers are cops

She is fourteen
and has been in a mental home for three
months, diagnosed as schizophrenic

She has been subject to many physical and
psychological investigations
She has a one-to-one psychotherapist
She attends group therapy
She attends occupational therapy
Her mother is seen by a social worker
The father and mother have seen one of the
psychiatrists several times
Her mother gets pills from her general
practitioner
There is a psychiatrist in charge of her in the
hospital
There is a psychiatrist in charge of her out of
the hospital

There is a consensus among all family members
that she was sent to the hospital for the following reasons:

She sat in her room and stared at the wall	while she should have been downstairs with the rest of the family watching television
She starved herself	She picked from the fridge and drank two pints of milk a day, but refused to eat 'meals' cooked by her mother
She was half the weight she should be	She seemed rather skinny; the rest of the family seemed twice the weight they should be
She washed her hands and face in cold water	instead of hot water like everyone else
She wanted to go out of the house if she couldn't stare at the wall	It was a family, they said, of 'hollerers'; everyone wanted to be the boss. The streets were not safe for her
She couldn't stand the shouting and the noise and found she could get away from it by staring at a wall	Her mother felt that by doing so, she might 'slip away' from her
She felt she was made fun of at school because she was skinny	She actually was. But they did not want to upset her by admitting she was right
She wanted to stay on at school	They felt it would be kinder to her if they took her away from school

I am sure that I have stared at walls for many
more hours than this girl.

In some circles this is called meditation – a way
of resting, calming, emptying, tranquillizing the mind. It seems
to me one of the natural functions, like sleeping, dreaming,
waking, being interested in things. Like breathing in and
breathing out, systole and diastole, open and close.

> She couldm't stand the noise – neither would I,
>> I expect
> she couldn't go out in the street
> she couldn't concentrate on her homework
>> very difficult

She had come across a normal natural resource,
cultured out of her subculture.

There may have been a competent meditation
teacher (someone who has spent years and *years* staring at a
wall, or nothing in particular) in town . . .

However, instead of this being viewed as a
possible avenue of temporary escape (the best action in some
situations is to escape – this is not escap–ism), and a refuge
(desperately and justifiably needed), this is regarded as the
prime symptom of a schizophrenic illness.

Her family are not sent off to an installation of the
medical–industrial complex in order to be reserviced so as
not to spend their time watching television.

I am told 'the average Canadian' watches television for five hours a day.

Would they be any the worse for staring at a
blank wall for five hours a day, I wonder?

> But moreover (to be fair),
> 'she is a case of day–night reversal'
> this is another ominous symptom of mental
> disorder
> and has to be stopped
> that is,

she is awake at night when it is quiet and tries to
get away from the fighting and bawling when the rest of the
family is awake and 'at it'.

The point is that she is 'out of control'. Her social
programming is breaking down, it might never even have

'taken'. She might have some genetic defect that renders her
more difficult to be socialized than her brothers, the cops, for
instance.

> She does not eat what is cooked for her
> or at the right time
> She does not sleep when she should
>   when it is normal for a girl
>   of her age to sleep
>   when all the other girls in her
>   class are asleep
> She does not wash her hands and face
> in hot water, like everyone else
>
> does this not show signs of negativism,
> of *asocial*, if not *anti*-social conduct
>
> She does not speak when spoken to, sometimes
> She is sometimes in tears
> because she is teased at
> school for being skinny
>
> does this not show signs of social
> maladaptation: even social manipulation,
> suggesting an hysterical
> psychopathology, rather than a
> schizophrenic?
>
> Her mother is desperately worried
> about her, slipping away from her
> not getting her proper food
> not getting her proper sleep
> and the social shame (it must be admitted) of her
> daughter becoming the laughing stock

but the *girl* is not	she shows no insight despite
worried	her selfish tears, she seems
she does not see why her	to be lacking in some, it is
mother should be worried	difficult to put one's finger
	on it precisely, but you *must*
	know what I mean, some lack
	of affect, of feeling;

indifference, or worse, more
suggestive of schizophrenia
than hysteria, although we
need not draw rigid lines.

just looking at her
she looks very healthy,
her skin is the only one of
the family that is not thick,
sallow, and greasy

schizophrenics may 'look'
healthier, physically, than
normal, and often *are* more
resistant to infections, some
say

her eyes are bright and alive
instead of being cancelled
like everyone else's
in fact she is rather fidgety

possibly hypomanic elements
or

a trace of catatonic even
hebephrenic features

she says she wants to be left
alone and be allowed to go
back to school
that the hospital is making
her worse
and she has now lost all her
friends

sounds as though she is
beginning to rationalize her
own failures and to be
developing,
typically,
a paranoid
inflection to her thinking

In view of the above 'treatment' – the inverse
isometric diametric opposite of therapy – consists of
1.   hospitalization   against her wish she is put away
                                in order to be prevented
                                from slipping away

2.   early prevention, arrest of pathological process
       by
(i)   stopping her staring at the wall
        instead of letting her, even encouraging her
(ii) stopping her finding tranquillity,
        by giving her 'tranquillizers'.
(iii) damaging her brain, and disordering her mind,
        by giving her a course of electric shocks (eight)
(iv) chemically gripping her puberty,
        by hormones

to induce menstruation and pump up the
development of her breasts because she may be
organically retarded in maturing (as
'schizophrenics' are often supposed to be).

She has not *complained* about these matters, but
she cannot be expected to know what to complain
about, otherwise why would she be in the hospital?

It is likely that she has an 'unconscious' sense of
failure and inferiority because she has not been
'dated' and tumbled by any boys, because her
breasts have not developed and she has not
menstruated.

Besides she is not *interested* in boys. By chemically inducing sexual changes, she might be
given a biological 'thrust' in an outward direction
at a critical moment in her life cycle.

7 Oct. 1973, London

male TV commentator (middle-aged):

'. . . she won a few races last year
then she had twins
and of course
twins are no good for racing
so they were got rid of,

and now she's racing again
and I make her the favourite for this race
and the very best of luck to her,
now,
and in her future career . . .'

I thought at first he was talking about
a woman athlete
but he was talking about a racehorse
However,
a racehorse today
a woman
          tomorrow
                    what's the difference?

10   The Scientific Method and Us

> Those that would gain what is under heaven by
> tampering with it –
> I have seen that they do not succeed. For that
> which is under heaven is like a holy vessel,
> dangerous to tamper with.
> Those that tamper with it, harm it.
> Those that grab it, lose it.

*Tao Te Ching**

'I used to be an obstetrician,' Dr William Masters
said, 'which is boring 90 per cent of the time. So every time
I delivered a boy I used to engage in a little contest to see if I
could cut the cord before he had an erection. I won about
50 per cent of the time.'†

The scientific method is based on tampering with
what would be happening if we were doing nothing to it.
Scientific interference is the most destructive
interference. Only a scientist knows *how* to interfere most
destructively.

Love reveals *facts* which, without it, remain
undisclosed.

* Translated by Arthur Waley, George Allen and Unwin, London,
1965.

† *International Herald Trbune,* Paris, 7 May 1973, p. 6.

A heartless intellect can do no other than investigate the hell of its own hellish constructions by its own hellish instruments/instrumentality/methods, and to describe, in the language of hell
its own hellish conclusions/findings/hypotheses.

The cure comes from the medicine,
and the art of medicine
originates in charity.

Hence,
to be cured is not a work of Faith,
but one of sympathy.

The true ground of medicine
is love.

Paracelsus*

We should not needlessly multiply (hypothetical) entities seems to be an excellent principle.†
In modern scientific theory and practice, an attitude is often encountered which takes its justification from this principle, but which I do not believe has anything to do with it.
This is, to discount the *existence* of X because we have no hypothesis to account for it, or because science has not verified it, or because science cannot prove it, and sometimes, even, because science cannot *dis*prove it.
Or again, to see no value in X, because present scientific theory cannot find any value in it.
Some scientists are unable to conceive that by their methods they screen out the type of information they do not want, in order to bring into outline the type of information they do.

* Quoted by Henry M. Pachter, *Paracelsus: Magic into Science*, Collier Books, New York, 1961, pp. 121, 152.
† Occam's razor: 'Entia non sunt multiplicanda praeter necessitatem.'

However if they look at the scientific information they get, forgetting to look at it in the light of the fact that the net of the scientific method does not actually catch the ocean upon which it is cast, they reduce themselves to intellectual idiocy.

Here is a well-known neuroscientist who has for years specialized in cutting the brains of California housewives in two, showing how his two hemispheres work after his years of research.*

'Space in the intracranial region is tight, and one wonders if the premium item could not have been utilized for better things than the kind of right-left duplication that now prevails. Evolution, of course, has made notable errors in the past, and one suspects that in the elaboration of the higher brain centers evolutionary progress is more encumbered than aided by the bilateralized scheme which, of course, is deeply entrenched in the mechanisms of development and also in the basic wiring plan of the lower nerve centres.' Sperry added that he felt the human head could probably do very well with a 'single unified set of brain controls'.

'With the existing cerebral system,' he said, 'most memories have to be laid down twice – one engram for the left hemisphere and another engram copy for the right hemisphere. The amount of information stored in memory in a mammalian brain is a remarkable thing in itself; to have to double it all for the second hemisphere would seem in many ways a bit wasteful. It is doubtful that all this redundancy has had any direct survival value. . .'

I sometimes feel, in reviewing the evidence on the localization of the memory trace, that the necessary conclusion is that learning just is not possible. It is difficult to conceive of a mechanism which can satisfy the conditions set for it. Nevertheless, *in spite of such evidence against it* [italics mine], learning does sometimes occur.

K. S. Lashley, 'In Search of the Engram' (1950)†

* R. W. Sperry, quoted by Leonard A. Stevens, *Explorers of the Brain*, Alfred A. Knopf, New York, 1971, p. 306.
† Quoted by L. A. Stevens, op. cit., p. 293.

Nevertheless

We are beginning to have some reasonable guesses as to the 'gadgets' [still in quotation marks] that would serve as a memory mechanism – guesses sufficiently concrete to permit testing by rigorous experimentation. I think it is realistic to hope for *an understanding of memory precise enough to permit experimental modification of it in men.*

Ralph Gerard (1953)*

There we go.

Half the patients in all hospitals in the United States are there for trouble in their brains. In Illinois a third of all State hospital inhabitants have senile psychoses. Pray for their speedy death or legislate for euthanasia, but waste no tears on them. They had their chance.

Everything we learn of organisms leads us to conclude not merely that they are analogous to machines but that they are machines. Man-made machines are not brains, but brains are a very ill-understood variety of computing machines. Cybernetics has helped to pull down the wall between the great world of physics and the ghetto of the mind.

So long as we, like good empiricists, remember that it is an act of faith to believe our senses, that we corrupt but do not generate information, and that our most reputable hypotheses are but guesses open to refutation, so long may we 'rest assured that God has not given us over to thraldom under that mystery of iniquity, of sinful man aspiring to the place of God'.†

No we may not (rest assured).

---

* *Readings from Scientific American Psychobiology,* W. H. Freeman, San Francisco, 1967.

† Warren S. McCulloch, *Embodiments of Mind,* MIT Press, Cambridge, Mass., 1965, pp. 276, 163, 164.

11   A Lecture

Charles Sherrington, one of the great physiologists of the early twentieth century, proposed that man is a
biochemical complex with certain ways of its own, but chemical
nonetheless. His major work in physiology consisted of the
exploration of the reflex arc and the attempt to establish the
nature and function of the central nervous system. In his major
technical monograph on the subject (*The Integrative Action of
the Nervous System*), he proposed that our nervous system
serves the function of integrating the different parts of itself
and of the body. In his Gifford lectures, 'Man on His Nature',
he took as an epigraph a quotation from Samuel Taylor
Coleridge, in which Coleridge speaks of the nature of an organism as a system in which the whole is implied in each of the
parts. Sherrington's method was vivisection, a method that
goes back in the West at least to the Greeks. Galen came
across a man who could move his body around without any
apparent impediment, but who had lost his sensory feedback.
He then showed experimentally that there were two sets of
pathways in the body, and postulated that there must be a set
of nerves going out (motor) and a set of nerves coming in
(sensory). The idea was that nerves were very thin tubes, and
something flowed along them in different directions. In order
to confirm his clinical observations 'scientifically', Galen cut
the spinal column of an animal into longitudinal sections (the
front, the side, the back of it, and so on), and established that
if these cuts were done in different places, there would be
different responses from the animal. That is, he cut a live
animal into slices, and did things to the slices to see what
would happen.

People who have never been through medical school themselves can't quite imagine what separates doctors from the rest of humanity. Exposure to this sort of stuff in practice is one of the things that definitely changes anyone over the years. In our physiology course, our first practical experiment was with frogs in a laboratory in which there were about fifty to sixty students arranged along benches. Half that number of live frogs had been set out, and when our instructor gave us the word, we had to take up these live frogs by their feet, and holding them like that, smash their heads simultaneously on the edge of the lab benches. First we observed what that did to a frog. It's been killed, but it still twitches. Then we systematically proceeded in a way that is described – I can't help saying beautifully, though it still absolutely freezes my heart when I read it – by William James in the first chapter of his *Principles of Psychology*.

I want to explore the relation between my mind and my brain. How shall I go about it? William James* tells me that 'the best way to enter the subject' is 'to take a lower creature, like a frog', and study, by cutting it up *alive* into different bits, 'the functions of his different nerve-centres'. If you play around with the bits attached to the spinal cord alone, their movements 'almost resemble in their machine-like regularity the performance of a jumping-jack, whose legs must twitch whenever you pull the string'.

If, then, we reduce the frog's nervous system to the spinal cord alone, by making a section behind the base of the skull, between the spinal cord and the medulla oblongata, thereby cutting off the brain from all connection with the rest of the body, the frog will still continue to live, but with a very peculiarly modified activity. It ceases to breathe or swallow; it lies flat on its belly, and does not, like a normal frog, sit up on its fore paws, though its hind legs are kept, as usual, folded against its body and immediately resume this position if drawn out. If thrown on its back, it lies there quietly, without turning over like a normal frog. Locomotion and voice seem entirely abolished. If we suspend it by the nose, and irritate

* *The Principles of Psychology*, Dover, New York, 1950, vol. I, pp. 14–19.

different portions of its skin by acid, it performs a set of
remarkable 'defensive' movements calculated to wipe away
the irritant. Thus, if the breast be touched, both fore paws will
rub it vigorously; if we touch the outer side of the elbow, the
hind foot of the same side will rise directly to the spot and
wipe it. The back of the foot will rub the knee if that be
attacked, whilst if the foot be cut away, the stump will make
ineffectual movements, and then, in many frogs, a pause will
come, as if for deliberation, succeeded by a rapid passage of
the opposite unmutilated foot to the acidulated spot. . .
          . . . The segment governing the arms is especially
active, in male frogs, in the breeding season; and these
members alone with the breast and back appertaining to
them, everything else being cut away, will then actively grasp
a finger placed between them and remain hanging to it for a
considerable time.

          And the same sort of thing in man. 'Robin, on
tickling the breast of a criminal an hour after decapitation,
saw the arm and hand move towards the spot.'
          The upper centres give orders to the lower
centres through a line of command.
          'It is like a general ordering a colonel to make a
certain movement, but not telling him how it shall be done.'
          I hope if someone wanted to get to know me he
would not bash me on the head, cut my brain out of my head,
take my head from my neck, cut my body in half, turn me
upside down, burn me with acid, and torture the whole and
all the bits with electricity and God knows what.
          There is a vogue nowadays of chopping up
worms into smaller and smaller bits, to see (among other
things) how many different bits will grow into new worms, who
are then chopped into bits, in turn, and so *ad infinitum.*

          I suppose I was fortunate as a student in Glasgow
to have as teachers a number of people who had established
themselves competently in this tradition. If we suppose that
we are bits of chemical matter of some kind, we've got to take
that flesh and blood and those nerves, and all the rest of it,

and simply do everything we can imagine to it and see how it responds. The idea is to take these bits of chemical stuff and torment and torture them in any way you like so long as you try to predict beforehand what will happen, on the basis of what has happened before. You hope to be able to predict what will happen if I do this on the basis of a hypothesis you've formed from what happened when you did that. If you're good at that and lucky, you may get a Nobel Prize. Sir Charles Sherrington put his stamp on the reflex arc, though he did not invent it, and the reflex arc is a figure indelibly imprinted on the mind of every medical student. And unless you have familiarized yourself with that kind of thing in biology and in physiology, anatomy, pathology, in clinical neurology, in neuropsychiatry, you haven't a chance of becoming a doctor; you'd never pass the exams. Sir Charles Sherrington says somewhere in *The Integrative Action of the Nervous System* that actually the reflex arc is an experimental 'fiction', and he points out that there are many others. This one is one of the exports of the laboratory into all our lives: much of the theory and practice of education, of the 'programming' of behaviour therapy, is based on the notion that we *basically*, when it comes down to it, after one has had the nerve to discard the untestable opinions of unscientific philosophers and others untutored in science, are physical-chemical black boxes; into this black box comes input, and out of it goes output. In between, some sort of central processing is going on, which is an elaboration of the in-between bits (which accounts for everything). Essentially, input comes in, is processed, and goes out.

The first piece of RAT research I came across was in the fifties. A biologist I knew was doing research with distant hopes of a Nobel Prize. Since he belonged to the left, he didn't think there was much chance of hitting a Nobel, though you never could tell. His work was to get rats under laboratory conditions and turn the heat down, colder and colder. The game was to see how cold you could get them before they would stop copulating. Now, he was a pure scientist, not an applied scientist. He had a permanent camera set up to film them 'at it'. Little bits of fluff would be given to them so that they could just warm themselves up a wee bit if they

huddled together as tightly as possible. Even after they were
deep-frozen stiff, when they got a little warmth back, they
would still make love.

      His was no trivial occupation. I often find it very
difficult to realize that probably every major government in the
world has stashed away, through vast underground labyrinths,
food for those people the computer determines as having
priority for survival at the last roundup. But the rats are a
menace because even in extreme cold, if there's still only
a little bit of something they can huddle in, they can still keep
it going. So it's a problem. Some of the so-called best, so-
called scientific, so-called minds are engaged in the rat race
for the Nobel Peace Prize on rat research.

      I once spent a lifetime (when I woke up and found
myself back in my bed, I couldn't decide for a while what was
dream and what was 'reality') as a rat in the sewers of contemporary Tokyo. I ended my rat lifetime in a way that my
rat consciousness couldn't make out, but it was something like
bubonic plague. I began to swell up. Pus was oozing out of
my blind eyes and all over the place. I staggered around,
then collapsed, faded out, and faded back into my bed.

      I must say, I preferred that death to the deaths
meted out to some people I've seen in our hospitals.

      I don't see how we can expect to get away with
tormenting our fellow creatures in the ways we do without this
evil method (practice) corrupting our ways of construing what
we are doing (theory). The Sherrington *et al.* examples typify
the 'pure' science of which clinical medicine is the applied
science. This is the basic theory, and it affects how we go
about 'seeing' and examining patients, whether it's general
examination and/or any of the presently recognized sub-
systems, when you can't find anything actually the matter with
any bit of a person, but the whole has gone haywire. The
theory conditions how we look at people, how we proceed
with people, and how we think about and talk about them (us)
among ourselves. The way people are 'treated' is the outcome of that theoretical position which one has to not only
internalize as input, but be fully fluent in as output. When we
'apply' such theory to humans, we, at our gentlest, most
humane, are led down the path of such procedures as 'be-

haviour modification'. The point of therapy is to get behaviour *out* of that sort of control (I should have thought), not to get it more efficiently technologically controlled.

When I was at medical school almost all my friends became psychiatrists, because it was the only bit of medicine we felt we could survive in, given the medico-surgical lunacy all round.

One is not allowed into the 'inner' circles of Western medicine in hospitals as a mere pre-clinical medical student. Once you are allowed in, you've passed a major landmark, and now you work in the hospital. If you want to, as I did, you can live in the hospital, perhaps for years. In my day the consulting surgeon came along, in pin-striped trousers and whatnot, on Monday morning and spoke to the registrar, also attired and moving in the appropriate manner, that pro-fessional bedside manner. He reminded me of Felix Krull, Thomas Mann's confidence trickster, who makes his way around different countries of Europe, with two or three words of French, two or three words of Italian, and gets by wherever he goes without having to say practically anything.

The Chief says, 'Well, what have we got in the ward today?' and the reply: 'Nothing but surgical trash, sir, I'm afraid. We've got a haemorrhoid in bed three, we've got a couple of veins, we've got a good gall bladder coming in tomorrow.'

'Ugh, ugh, what are we going to show the students?'

'Well, we've got a good anal prolapse. It doesn't have surgical interest, but it's a good teaching thing.' It actually happens like that.

Half a dozen or more students, for whom it's all new, follow him around the ward, all in white coats, all with stethoscopes and various other gadgets: 'Mr So-and-so, would you care to do a PR for us and tell us what you find on Mrs McLaughlin?' Mrs McLaughlin is, say, a woman of about fifty, who has come in because she's been losing a lot of weight and has abdominal pain. We were wondering if she might have a cancerous growth, and it will be interesting to see if one can feel it by putting a finger, with a rubber fitted around it, up her anus, and then moving it this way and that, noting when

she squeals with pain. I shall resist the temptation to tell
some of my medical horror stories. Every doctor has his batch.
There was a lot of genuine humanity among the doctors and
teachers and clinicians in Glasgow, but at its very best,
medical training was bedevilled, and still is, by its own insane
theory and insane practice. At least, so it seems to me. When
I got to psychiatry I started to read the clinical descriptions.
Schizophrenia, for instance. It is said to be characterized by
dissociated thought and feeling. Thought has become split
from feeling, and both have become disordered in a number
of ways. Either might fall apart and become incoherent,
or thought might become superorganized, systematized,
excessively coherent. Everything is accountable for. The
patient is said to be incapable of forming a relationship with
others on a personal basis, but can 'relate' only mechanically.
He or she is 'autistic'. Not only that but worse, *how* one thinks
is incorrigibly in error, impervious to reason, and dogmatic,
in the worst sense of the term. We expect to find among the
group of schizophrenics so-called 'catatonic' symptoms, which
means an inability to move oneself around in space except
in peculiar ways, in stilted, mechanical ways that look like the
movements of a robot, or some sort of machine. Then there's
a whole range of other things that may or may not be present
in various degrees. There are different ways of saying much
the same things. You always expect to find some 'depersonalization'; 'affective impoverishment', inability to form relationships, autism. The head (cognitive function) is divorced from
the heart. Textbooks describe inability to feel, lack of sight,
imperviousness, robotization, mechanization, the loss of sense
of feeling for quality, often self-confessed feelings of futility
and meaninglessness. 'Schizoid' individuals maybe have
'insight', but it is without feeling, it's heartless; thinking may
be precise, but it's without heart. When, as a medical student,
I came across these descriptions in medical textbooks for the
first time, I thought they were a very good description of
medicine itself, including psychiatry. The heartlessness, the
divorce, the split between head and heart. The fragmentation,
indeed disintegration, behind all that, and its disavowal and
projection. The unavailing cognitive efforts to put pieces
together. The 'institutionally reinforced' imperviousness of the

cognitive scheme, the self-perpetuating, self-confirming nature
of the process, which can never prove itself wrong by itself.
What is being described is not what it appears to be: the
description is largely of a reflection, as in a mirror, unrecog-
nized as such by those looking into the mirror and seeing
themselves.

There was one full-length mirror in my home as a
child, and I spent a lot of time looking into it. That's supposed
(in some quarters) to be an early symptom of schizophrenia,
or at least ominous. Along with many other things I did as a
child. Mirrors are very important. Winnicott proposes that
when a baby looks at its mother's face, the face is the baby's
first mirror. It's in that face that one sees oneself reflected.
The image one develops of one's own face is built up in very
complex ways. Once it is established, I suppose many people
feel they are somewhere or other behind a face which they
can't see because they are on this side of it, but if they could
see, if they could look into a mirror, or if they could get
around in their imagination from behind and look at themselves
from outside, then they would see their 'face'.

But what is one's original face before one is born?
This face that we take to be our face is far from our original
face, and if we identify ourselves with that face, then we're
already in a sense deracinated, uprooted, and captured by
this magic spell of reflected images reflecting each other,
wherein we can become lost by identifying ourselves with
any part of it. There's no way to describe one's original face.
One can only allude. Some people go so far as to try to char-
acterize their original face, but that is felt to be going too far
by those who have gone further.

If I felt shaky, scattered, unaccountably frightened,
or in any state of bewilderment or consternation or disarray
or perplexity or confusion, and if I went to many a mental
hospital looking for help, then I would be like the Aztecs
rushing into the mouths of the Spanish cannon in hope of
finding deliverance. If I really wanted to put myself in the
position of being driven crazy, then the best way I can think
of going about it is to go into one of those psychiatric institu-
tions, mental hospitals, where psychiatric psychosis is in full
swing, uncontested. In such places there is complete local

power to chop and cut people up, physically as well as theo-
retically, in the name of the exact opposite of what is said is
being done. The error in psychiatry is not just a casual one.
It's an error of one hundred and eighty degrees in the
opposite direction without insight.

I don't use psychiatric terms in my own theory
and practice. I find psychiatry in such entangled confusion
that personally I can do perfectly well without it. Many of its
severest critics have themselves been psychiatrists. If it deals
largely in fictions, these fictions are powerful social facts.
Concepts used as mandates to do things to people are facts,
like so many of the other facts of our social life : you could call
them factoids or pseudo-facts, like these other systems that
grab a sufficient number of people to become endemic and
then are accepted by perhaps the majority, for a time.

I do not assume that anyone who is diagnosed as
psychotic or anything else is, *per se*, *ipso facto*, more or less
crazy than the person – or computer – doing the diagnosing.

I am very interested in words, and what we
have words for and what we haven't got words for. For
instance, the word 'paranoia'. It always seems very strange to
me that we have this word which means, in effect, that someone feels that he is being persecuted when the people who
are persecuting him don't think that he is. But we haven't got
a word for the condition in which you are persecuting someone without realizing it, which I would have thought is as
serious a condition as the other, and certainly no less common.

Electroshock therapy was being tried out in
Glasgow when I was a medical student. Its introduction was
bitterly opposed by some of the senior psychiatrists, including
my first psychiatric teacher, Dr Sclare. He illustrated his
objections by citing the case of a woman of twenty-six who
had begun a career as a concert violinist. At the end of her
first, very successful tour she had crashed into a depression,
and it was felt it would be a pity if she didn't get going again
fairly soon. So she got a course of electric shocks, which
brightened her up. But unfortunately (one of the common side
effects of these things), she forgot her violin repertoire. At
least she couldn't remember it sufficiently to be able to play in

concerts any more – ever. In those days (1949), in Glasgow, most of the senior psychiatrists wouldn't have anything to do with electric shocks, but they are very appealing today because they do often brighten people up and get them going again, walking and talking. One enthusiast in London goes around publicly giving figures of 85 per cent remission of symptoms in electric shock treatment for involutional depression, and comparable figures for all sorts of other conditions, including children who don't want to have anything to do with other people, seventeen-year-old hysterics, and so on. He gets 'very good results' so far as I hear. He comes around in the morning, does the ward rounds. 'How are you today? Better or worse?' And if you don't say you're better, you get another course of electric shock treatment. Most people say they are better, and most of them do not report back to the out-patient department.

In the last couple of years I have visited, on invitation, a number of psychiatric establishments, such as Yale Psychiatric, Harvard Child Psychiatric, Illinois State, and similar places all over America; as well as having got involved somewhat in the goings on in psychiatric departments elsewhere from Banaras to New Zealand, even London. As a result, although not employed within a psychiatric institution, I remain in touch with what is currently going on.

I remember one case conference in which I 'presented', as a psychiatrist, a young man who was a patient at the Glasgow University Department of Psychiatry. The young man was suffering from a sense of futility. This is considered a symptom of schizoid personality disorder, along with derealization and depersonalization and so forth. He could find no meaning to life. After I'd given his 'history' and a short account of the patient, he was brought in and asked a few questions, and then sent out again. Around the table we (about a dozen psychiatrists, clinical psychologists, and social workers) discussed this 'case'. One question was the diagnosis, whether this patient was a schizoid personality, or whether he was possibly at the beginning of a schizophrenic process of deterioration. I ventured (this was in 1956) to remark that the question whether life was worth living had been taken up quite a bit in recent European literature, indeed one could find considerations of it all over the place. I did not think it was a foregone conclusion that the sense of futility betokened psychopathology.

After the conference the head of the department asked me to come to his office. He said that he thought there was something in what I said. Even he, a professor of psychiatry, could remember two occasions in his life when he had had 'attacks' of futility. One was when he was a colonel in the British army during the war, and was travelling a lot by train. As he looked out the window, very tired, he was overcome by a transient attack of futility. He put it down to the parallax phenomenon working on a fatigued CNS. His second attack had been when he was tying his left shoelace that very morning : as he bent down, he was overcome with a sense of futility. He is a very well-intentioned person, and I respect him and am fond of him, but he would rate in my book as in some respects more out of touch with reality than the patient was. (Psychiatrists are people as well as patients.) And so it is with so many people who are subjected to such an inundation of desperate people seeking their help, and feel helpless in the face of all this misery they are supposed to do something about. Such people are always dreaming of a 'breakthrough' in treatment.

When I was at the Glasgow Royal Mental Hospital, Gart Navel, I spent the best part of three months living, as much as I could, in the female refractory ward of the hospital. In that hospital, we had ladies' west and women's east and gentlemen's west and men's east, for the paying and nonpaying patients respectively. In the female east admissions ward, a locked ward with the usual paraldehyde and bromide sedatives, I persuaded the hospital authorities to try an experiment of taking everyone off every drug that they didn't want. Thirty windows in that ward were broken during the first week. All were replaced, as they were broken, by the hospital maintenance staff, who were very glad to have something to do. The cost of replacing the broken glass was, I think, less than one tenth the cost of the drugs that these people were usually put 'under'.

When tranquillizers came in, however, they
didn't smell like paraldehyde and didn't have the side effects
of bromide, and they seemed both to quiet people and to
make them more 'cooperative'. At a staff meeting with doctors
and nurses, one of the nursing sisters asked about a somewhat
wild woman. 'Do these new drugs have any effect on height?'
she wondered. We asked what she meant, and she reported
that she thought this woman had shrunk three inches since
she had been on tranquillizers. I said that to the best of my
knowledge, they didn't have any effect on height, but it was
an observation I've continued to remember. I've often been
asked by residents in hospitals to give a patient an injection
when there might be some sort of life starting up in him,
perhaps a crying or whimpering or yelling or screaming
or not going to bed at the proper time, not getting up at the
proper time, not coming to eat at the proper time, and so on.
Doctors often feel that there is nothing they can do except to
give the patient an injection to keep at least the staff calmer.
They're not always terribly happy about it.

There's nothing that affects our chemistry more
immediately than other people. When one walks into a room
where one feels welcome and comfortable and so on, if one had
a little trepidation before going in, that settles down, one's
heart is not in a flurry, one's breathing is calm, one's palms
are not sweating, one's throat isn't dry, one doesn't have
butterflies in one's stomach. All these experiential affairs
are inextricably part of the same tapestry as that of our
chemistry. There's nothing more intimately attuned to how we
feel in other people's company than our body chemistry.
And I'm sure that just as there is a chemistry of acute fear,
so there is a chemistry of chronic despair.

In the case of the wild woman, a chemical agent
had modified her behaviour, and there was a reportable,
measurable change in another person's perception, so that
that person experienced her as smaller. Transformations
induced by introducing a chemical agent inside the skin of one
person included perceptual changes in other people who
shared the same social system.

'Tranquillizers' are another import into our lives
from the laboratory. They were drugs found to help people

who were interested in controlling rats, rendering them more
amenable and more cooperative. Chemical agents that enable
rats to be controlled more efficiently are given to people for
the same reason. Given a suitable selling name first, of course.
You can't 'tranquillize' someone. Tranquillity cannot be
imposed by a chemical. In recent years in the USA I've often
been asked to 'do' an interview with a patient in front of other
people. I have sometimes agreed, with the stipulation that the
patient not be on tranquillizers. Out of the first eight occasions
set up that way, not one psychiatric department could bring
itself to present a patient to me who was regarded as psychotic
but not on tranquillizers. The staff seem ashamed and terrified
of anyone out of their control. In some quarters, as soon as
anyone starts to *feel* anything, then they've got to be very
careful just whom they tell, and how they go about mani-
festing it, and so on. According to my friend Ross Speck, who
was professor of psychiatry at the Hahnemann Medical
College in Philadelphia, the most common last straw leading
to admission to mental hospitals in the United States in 1972
was – what would you think? – smashing the television set!
      Gart Navel wasn't too bad as a genuine refuge.
Quite a few patients would admit themselves back there of
their own accord. The dictum, when it was set up in the nine-
teenth century, was *no injurious treatment*: no injury was to be
done to the patient in the name of his or her treatment – a
very important principle. It *was* an asylum for some people ;
it depended on who was 'running' what wards, of course.
      When I spent those months in the female refrac-
tory ward of the hospital, I did my other duties, but I spent
most of my time, day and night, in that ward. There were
about sixty patients, with two nurses at a time. A doctor exam-
ined each patient at statutory six-month intervals, when the
patient was tucked tightly into bed, with screens around. The
doctor would apply the stethoscope to see that she wasn't
dying of pneumonia, and get out again as quickly as possible.
It was impossible to ascertain how many people in that ward
had had lobotomies in the last few years ; they weren't even
down in the case records. After three or four weeks, I was
part of the life of that ward. No doctor ever entered the locked
door without the telephone ringing from another ward to say

that he was on his way. Then the nurse would come in and say, 'The doctor is coming', and everyone would take up their appropriate positions and start up their usual numbers. What the doctor then saw (including, presumably, the doctor who had been the superintendent of that hospital and who wrote one of the most commonly taught textbooks of psychiatry) bore little resemblance to what otherwise went on in that place.

After taking stock of this situation for three months, and being in full sympathy with the patients and with those nurses who took heart as soon as they saw just a possibility that this ghastly, dismal scene might possibly change, I wrote a report in which I put forward to the hospital management committee various recommendations for changing the different aspects of the institutional structure of the part of the hospital where I worked. In the first place, I pointed out that, in my view, it was quite clear from my observations that more important than my medication was the relationship between staff and patients, and the relationship between patients and other patients.

The nurses hadn't realized this themselves; they were taught that they had jobs to do, but that their 'jobs' didn't include being friendly with patients. They came on in shifts, were attached to a ward, and then might be shifted at a moment's notice to another ward. Say a nurse was getting along well with a few patients after being on one ward for a little while. She could disappear, never to appear again. She could be shifted without warning to another ward on the other side of the hospital, and that would be that. 'Her' patients were suddenly bereft of possibly their one lifeline to the outer world. Almost all the women had been locked up there for years. What they felt was considered meaningless, of course, because they're all crazy, that's why they're there. If their feelings were taken seriously, they couldn't be treated in the way they were (are).

I wrote a detailed, point-by-point report on the state of affairs at the hospital. I'd just come out of the British army where I was a captain and I wasn't frightened about being only twenty-five years old. I made a number of specific proposals of which several were adopted, and there was one

that involved myself specifically. Sitting in the refractory ward,
I concentrated on those people who were regarded as the
most hopeless, who had been given up completely. I ascer-
tained from the nurses whom they felt most hopeless about,
and noted also whom the nurses and other patients left most
alone, and who made fewest moves themselves toward others.
All of the people on the ward had been hospitalized continually for at least six years, all of them were over thirty-five,
and all were women. I drew up sociograms of the interplay of
relationships on the ward, and I answered my own questions
as to the most hopeless patients, the most withdrawn, the
patients who were the most neglected, those whom other
patients had least to do with, and those who reacted least and
did least.

The twelve most hopeless patients were selected
by these criteria. There were a couple of other people on the
hospital staff at the time who also were hopeful about change,
including the assistant matron. It was agreed that these
twelve patients would have two nurses whose sole duty, I
insisted, would be to have them as their flock. It wasn't
possible to obtain all of the conditions I'd hoped for, but what
was possible was to have these two nurses assigned on a
promise for at least a year, if they wanted to stick it out, to be
with these patients from nine in the morning till five at night.
The hours were at the matron's insistence. And not on week-
ends. I said to the nurses that I wasn't going to worry about
whether they went on duty at nine or left at five – you can't
do these things that way – but that they should just be with
these people as much as they could take. If they couldn't
take it, this should not cost them promotion, loss of face, or so
on. The other stipulation was that the patients have their own
room. I couldn't get a twenty-four-hour-a-day room, but I did
get a rather pleasant room, simply laid out. It wasn't a ward;
there were no beds in it. And so the twelve patients and two
nurses went to that room from nine in the morning till five in
the evening.

On the first day, the twelve 'completely withdrawn' patients had to be shepherded from the ward across
to the day room. The second day, at half past eight in the
morning, I had one of the most moving experiences of my life

on that ward. There they all were clustered around the locked door, just waiting to get out and get over there with the two nurses and me. And they hopped and skipped and twiddled around and whatnot on their way over. So much for being 'completely withdrawn'.

I left that hospital about a year later. The project was continued, in modified form, after I left. In eighteen months from the start, all twelve patients had left the hospital. In another year all twelve were back again. The experiment petered out, but at the time it made a difference to the twelve people and two nurses, and to a lot of others. Many other aspects of the hospital took on a somewhat different complexion to the staff. Nothing succeeds like success. It worked while it lasted, and did not cost anything.

Today, they're cutting up children and putting devices into unborn babies. The statistics for the number of women to men whose brains have been cut up in America are 3 to 1, all *by* men. About twenty generations back in Europe, 100,000 women a year, a very large percentage of the population in those days, were being picked up in their beds in the middle of the night, without warning, stripped of all their clothes, thrown into a cart, and then trundled off into the inquisitorial European dungeons. There, after starvation and kicking about a bit, they'd be subject to torture, interrogation, and burning. Twenty generations back, that's what was going on. And this was not reported in the newspapers, you know. These women came from all classes, from the top to the bottom of the social structure, your grannies and mine, grannies grannies grannies, sometimes young girls, sometimes aged, married or single, tortured and burnt. This is just to put a little bit of social and historical perspective on what's happening now. It's done so neatly today that most people don't know it's happening.

Respect, courtesy, gentleness, kindness, consideration, compassion, charity: I believe we all know what these terms mean. They do not preclude technique and technology. Over twenty years ago, in my humble capacity as a young doctor, one of my jobs was to keep brain-dead human heart-lung 'preparations' alive longer than anyone else. A surgical team (was it in Stockholm or Tokyo?) had kept someone with almost total erasure of the brain, even with a lot of midbrain damage, alive for a couple of years. I don't know whether one would say 'alive' or not. If you are sufficiently smart at this, with appropriate 'drips' and so forth, you can keep the heart pumping and the lungs going on almost indefinitely it seems, just for, as we would say, the sake of science. The game was playing with human flesh to see who would have the best report to make at the next International Congress of Neurosurgery.

Such technology is demonic, but technology needn't be like that. We can have all the technology we want, and have it even much more precise, more accurate, and much better than we've got, and put it all into the woodwork when we want it, as a back-up for life, not to mangle life by it, or to turn ourselves into very inefficient computers. I wouldn't even try to compete with computers or with anything that a computer does, any more than I would try to compete with a crane. I can't do that. But to be sent to school and university and medical school in order to turn oneself into a very inefficient type of computer is total nonsense. We can have the technology, but if it's heartless, forget it. Speaking about being openhearted is not a matter of being 'romantic' or 'back-to-nature' or 'humanities' or any other of the stereotypes people sometimes respond with if one talks about the heart. It's a matter of common sense, God help us all.

Old and New Information about Electroshock

Ugo Cerletti M.D.*

Convulsions were to be induced with a therapeutic aim since the good clinical results obtained by Meduna's method were ascribed to them. For this the old transcranial method followed by physiologists was sufficient. But this idea then, and for a long time to come, appeared Utopian, because of the terror with which the notion of subjecting a man to high-tension currents was regarded. The spectre of the electric chair was in the minds of all and an imposing mass of medical literature enumerated the casualties, often fatal,

* *American Journal of Psychiatry*, 107 /2, August 1950, pp. 87–94.

ensuing upon electric discharges across the human body.
Nowadays, after twelve years of experience with electroshock, that terror may seem to have been exaggerated; but
cases of death caused by low tensions (forty volts) had been
described. Since, to obtain fits in dogs, tensions of around 125
volts were used, moreover with an alternating current –
which was held to be more dangerous than direct – it seemed
evident that these experiments were too near the danger zone
to have any possibility of being applied to man. The fact is that
no one at the clinic seriously thought of applying electric
convulsions *to man*, even though experiments continued upon
dogs, both with electricity and with Cardiazol. So, over a year
went by.

Nevertheless I, who had gone to such lengths
in striving to preserve dogs from death when given electri-
cally induced convulsions, had now come to the conviction
that a discharge of electricity must prove equally harmless to
a man if the duration of the current's passage were reduced
to a minimum interval. Continually turning the problem over
in my mind I felt that I would sooner or later be able to solve
it; so much so that in 1937, not being able to go to the Mun-
singen Congress, I allowed Bini to hint at these vague hopes,
and I, myself, at the 1937 Milan Assembly concerning the
therapeutics of schizophrenia, announced these hopes that I
had been nourishing.

This inactivity in the face of so momentous a
question greatly depressed me, so that I immediately jumped
at the information, given me by my colleague, Professor Vanni,
that 'at the Rome slaughterhouse pigs are killed by electricity'.
As though to justify my passiveness and to settle my hopes by
facing a real fact, I decided to see this electric slaughtering
with my own eyes, and immediately went to the slaughterhouse.

There I was told that the application of a current
across the pigs' heads had been in use for some years. The
butchers took hold of the pigs near their ears with a large
scissor-shaped pair of pincers. The pincers were connected
to the lighting plant with wires, and terminated in two teethed
disc-electrodes enclosing a sponge wet with water. As they
were seized, the pigs fell on their sides and were soon taken

by fits (convulsed). Then the butcher, taking advantage of the unconscious state of the animal, gave its neck a deep slash, thus bleeding it to death.

I at once saw that the fits were the same as those I had been producing in dogs, and that these pigs were not being 'killed by electricity', but were bled to death during the epileptic coma.

Since a great number of pigs was available at the slaughterhouse for killing, I now set myself the exact opposite of my former experiments' aims; namely, no longer to make efforts to keep the convulsed animals alive, but rather to determine what the conditions must be for obtaining their death by an electric current. Having obtained authorization for experimenting from the director of the slaughterhouse, Professor Torti, I carried out tests, not only subjecting the pigs to the current for ever-increasing periods of time, but also applying the current in various ways: across the head, across the neck, and across the chest. Various durations (twenty, thirty, sixty or more seconds) were tried. It turned out that the more serious results (prolonged apnea sometimes lasting many minutes and, exceptionally, death) appeared when the current crossed the chest; that this application was not mortal for durations of some tenths of a second; and, finally, that passage of the current across the head, even for long durations, did not have serious consequences. It was found that pigs, even when treated in this last way several times, 'came to' gradually, after a fairly long interval (five to six minutes), then started moving, next made various attempts to get shakily to their feet, and finally ran rapidly to mix with their mates in the pen.

These clear proofs, certain and oft repeated, caused all my doubts to vanish, and without more ado I gave instructions in the clinic to undertake, next day, the experiment upon man. Very likely, except for this fortuitous and fortunate circumstance of pigs' pseudo-electrical butchery, electroshock would not yet have been born.

A schizophrenic of about forty, whose condition was organically sound, was chosen for the first test. He expressed himself exclusively in an incomprehensible gibberish made up of odd neologisms, and since his arrival from

Milan by train without a ticket, not a thing had been ascertainable about his identity.

Preparations for the experiment were carried out in an atmosphere of fearful silence bordering on disapproval in the presence of various assistants belonging to the clinic and some outside doctors.

As was our custom with dogs, Bini and I fixed the two electrodes, well wetted in salt solution, by an elastic band to the patient's temples. As a precaution, for our first test, we used a reduced tension (seventy volts) with a duration of 0.2 second. Upon closing the circuit, there was a sudden jump of the patient on his bed with a very short tensing of all his muscles; then he immediately collapsed onto the bed without loss of consciousness. The patient presently started to sing at the top of his voice, then fell silent. It was evident from our long experience with dogs that the voltage had been held too low.

I, bearing in mind the observations with repeated applications of the day before upon pigs, made arrangements for a repetition of the test.

Someone got nervous and suggested whisperingly that the subject be allowed to rest; others advised a new application to be put off to the morrow. Our patient sat quietly in bed, looking about him. Then, of a sudden, hearing the low-toned conversation around him, he exclaimed – no longer in his incomprehensible jargon, but in so many clear words and in a solemn tone – 'Not a *second*. Deadly!'

The situation was such, weighted as it was with responsibility, that this warning, explicit and unequivocal, shook the persons present to the extent that some began to insist upon suspension of the proceedings, Anxiety lest something that amounted to superstition should interfere with my decision urged me on to action. I had the electrodes reapplied, and a 110-volt discharge was sent through for 0.5 second. The immediate, very brief cramping of all the muscles was again seen; after a slight pause, the most typical epileptic fit began to take place. True it is that all had their hearts in their mouths and were truly oppressed during the tonic phase with apnea, ashy paleness, and cadaverous facial cyanosis – an apnea which, if it be awe-inspiring in a spontaneous epileptic fit, now seemed painfully never-ending – until at the first deep, stertorous inhalation, and first clonic shudders, the blood ran more freely in the bystanders' veins as well; and, lastly, to the immense relief of all concerned, was witnessed a character-istic, gradual awakening 'by steps'. The patient sat up of his own accord, looked about him calmly with a vague smile, as though asking what was expected of him. I asked him: 'What has been happening to you?' He answered, with no more gibberish: 'I don't know; perhaps I have been asleep.'

That is how the first epileptic fit experimentally induced in man through the electric stimulus took place. So electroshock was born; for such was the name I forthwith gave it. . .

Bini in 1942 suggested the repetition of ECT many times a day for certain patients, naming the method 'annihilation'. This results in severe amnesic reactions that ap-pear to have a good influence in obsessive states, psychogenic depressions and even in some paranoid cases. 'Clustering' of treatments, shocking daily for three or four days followed by a three-day rest, is less intense but sometimes effectual. The method of annihilation has made possible studies of amnesia and of hallucinations, delirium, and moria occurring during the treatment, relating them to the personality factors in the patients (Bini and Bazzi, Polimanti). Flescher and Virgili have made systematic researches on amnesia and showed that spontaneous memory is more damaged than that of learned, didactic material and that automatic memory is still less disturbed. Depressed and aged patients show disturbances earlier than young or excited patients. The 'annihilation syndrome' has been compared by Cerquetelli and Catalano with the psychopathology following prefrontal leukotomy. They indicate close parallelism with the advantage of reversi-bility in the case of shcok.

These authors have also used shock successively to stop the symptoms of demerol mania quickly, following Martinotti who used it with success in other forms of toxi-comania. Broggi and others have also used ECT in progres-sive paralysis with at least temporary success. Ruggeri has used ECT in Parkinsonism and DeCrinis in disseminated sclerosis, observing attenuation of hypertonia.

Electroshock has also been applied in certain general physical illnesses though all have a constitutional 'nervous' background. Recovery has been frequently reported in asthma, and Catalano and Cerquetelli, with Tommasi, have had success in psoriasis, prurigo, and alopecia areata. Mancioli, after having observed improvement in ozena in a schizophrenic patient treated with shock, found similar improvement after acroagonine injection and is pursuing the research with histological controls.

Two other ideas both of which have perhaps as much relation to poetry as to science must be mentioned. The first is simply that the word 'shock' does not have the same meaning in neuropsychiatry as in general pathology. It is worth noting that many of our therapeutic methods such as prolonged sleep, narcoanalysis, insulin coma, epileptic coma, electronarcosis, etc., have in common the factor of the induction of a state of unconsciousness.

The second idea has to do with the patient's fear of therapy, which leads some to want to stop it. On being asked the reason, they reply: 'I don't know, I am afraid.' 'Afraid of what?' 'I don't know, I have fear.' 'But were you worried, did you feel pain?' 'No, but I have fear.' There must be a vague recollection – organic memory – of the first 'terror-defence' reaction. I believe that name 'terror-defence' expresses the biological significance of epileptic fits. The terror phase, although taking place during unconsciousness, leaves specific bio-chemical and psychological changes in the organism that later emerge generically into the conscious sphere. This, too, was expressed long ago by Padre Dante,

'Qual e colui che somniando vede,
E dope il sogno la passione impressa
Rimane, e l'altro alla mente non riede. . .
(Para. XXXIII, 58–61)

(As he who while dreaming sees,
And after the dream is over,
The emotion remains while the picture has
    faded away. . .)

12   Field Notes

14 Nov. 1972, Cafeteria, Buffalo Airport. c. 9.00 am

Black Waitress	(to white man who is bugging her) put me into the black void
	where you will not bother me
Me	put you where?
She	the black void. V–O–I–D. void.
	from where you are reborn
Me	black?
She	that's how I picture it
Me	do you remember it?
She	just as I picture it, sir.

12 Nov. 1972

Notice in New York taxicab
No smoking
Driver allergic

Me	(to lady taxidriver) ten years ago there would have been something the matter with you, if you couldn't stand your lungs being poisoned
She	yeah. Not now. It's a filthy habit
Me	why do you think people smoke?
She	it's a detensifier
Me	oh. How do you mean?
She	they have to have something in their mouths
Me	why?

She	I think it's a habit from the breast, maybe they didn't get enough of it then. Of course I'm not a so-called expert. But that's what I think. What do you think?
Me	yes I think it's something like that. Seems very likely to me.

21 Nov. 1972, The Manger, Tampa, Florida
7.30 pm

An extensive lawn in the hotel grounds, of dark green *plastic* (!) grass.

28 Nov. 1972, Hotel Utah, Salt Lake City

Danny and I began to get desperate for some real food

all the milk is homogenized
all the fruit is chemicalized
nothing but dyed buttermilk
the cheeses are all chemicalized one way or another

just a mouthful of real bread, at least.

we scoured the town in a taxi. Taken to (according to the taxi driver) the only health food shop in town

only frozen, presliced 'health-food' bread, in cellophane

1 Dec. 1972, New Orleans

Saved. Food at last. Real coffee at last.

14 Nov. 1972, in flight Buffalo to Chicago

Stewardess	are you R. D. Laing?
Me	yes
Stewardess	I majored in psychology at Duke

Me	really
Stewardess	are you interested in ESP?
Me	well, er, I sort of grew up with it in Scotland
Stewardess	do you think it's been *cultured out*?
Me	I haven't heard that expression before
Stewardess	cultured out?
Me	maybe, maybe not forever

2 Dec. 1972, in flight New Orleans to Washington

I had taken my shoes and socks off.

Stewardess	(indicating my feet) is anything the matter sir?
Me	no
Stewardess	I'm sorry there is a regulation that all passengers must have adequate covering over their feet
Me	oh I'm sorry. Excuse me. I didn't know (putting on shoes and socks)
Stewardess	thank you sir
Me	I didn't know there was such a regulation

We developed a friendly chat. She told me that since a little girl she had never ever allowed her bare feet to touch the ground or the earth, neither bathing, nor coming out of a bath, nor going in and out of bed.

11 Oct. 1973, Venice c. 10.00 am

A clutch of affluent women, with clichéd faces
one of them spots a shop window,
with barely a glance at the window,
she calls out:

1st Woman	Mabel, come here, it's fantastic!!
Mabel	(goes over, and turns her glutted eyes to the window: a clear moment *before* her eyes have contacted the window display, she shouts out) *fantastic!!!*

I used this vignette in several lectures to illustrate
the thesis that we live within, or can easily come to live within,
a skein of words,
        such that we see, as it were, other people's
descriptions of the world,
        instead of describing what we see. Other people
(like the first woman) are not 'seeing' the world either, very
often.
        the map is not the territory,
        the menu is not the meal, etc.
but that mote in one's own eye(s)!

Jutta	(driving through fantastic scenery)
	isn't it fantastic scenery
Me	(with cursory turn of head) *fantastic!*

Natasha	(new dress) do you like it?
Me	(writing) yes, it's very nice
Natasha	how do you know? You haven't seen it yet
	(I had forgotten to look up)

28 Jan. 1973, Auckland to Honolulu 11.30 am

He used to be an obstetrician, he tells me. Now
he is the Chief of the Research and Development Department
of one of the transworld chemical industries. His department
has a thirty-six million dollar a year budget.
        employs ninety-eight PhDs, and over thirty
        MDs, and in addition, gives
        grants for research to many university depart-
        ments throughout the world.

        We were introduced in the First Class Airport
Lounge by the host, and are now sitting together, knocking
back Scotch on the rocks.

He is very interested in the chemical key to schizophrenia. Feels a breakthrough may not be far off. Has noted my name in the bibliographies. One of his daughters said to him he ought to read some of my stuff.

He	I have two daughters. I've trained them both not to be interested in sex. Both are 'top' in their different academic fields now.
Me	are they?
He	what?
Me	interested in sex?
He	no. Both are safely married. I used to be a surgeon. I gave it up. But I do what I can from where I'm at.
Me	you must have gone through the Second World War then
He	it was disheartening, yes. That had something to do with it. Were you in it?
Me	I just missed it. I learned my neurology from a chap who had been Chief of the British Army's No. 1 Field Brain Surgery Unit through Africa and Italy. Eighteen hours a day sometimes.
He	I was in Burma. We had a Jap brought in. We offered a thousand dollars for a live Jap. They were wanted for interrogation.
Me	offered to whom?
He	the boys. Almost impossible to get one in alive. This one already had four punctures from bayonets in his stomach. But he was alive. So they got their thousand dollars. They 'interrogated' him and got what they wanted. I spent three and a half hours resecting yards of bowel, etc. He was carried out on a stretcher. Two shots. The sergeant came in and saluted: 'Prisoner shot trying to escape sir.'
Me	that's it
He	that's it (another couple of Scotches on the rocks)
He	our speciality was assembling and wrapping up our Surgical Theatre tent in twenty minutes

	two hundred million people suffer from schisto-somiasis – ten years' expectancy
Me	I didn't know that
He	one hundred per cent of the population behind two of the big dams suffer from it
Me	really?
He	yes we have developed a drug. It's less toxic than the parasite. We laid out the red carpet for two ministers of health. Told them about it. They didn't want to know. Said it would land them with overpopulation.
Me	so?
He	R & D is all right. But we have to have a market.
Me	sure
He	no one would bite. Hell. I thought that was a shame. I thought if we could just do one production run – the stuff would at least be there.
Me	no buyers
He	we did do one run. The American Army funded it. In case they might wish to move their troops sometime into a schistosomiasis area. The stuff's there. That's all I could do.
	(another two Scotches)
	you're a psychiatrist?
Me	yes
He	you know that one about the guy who goes into the same bar every evening for twenty years and has two drinks?
Me	no
He	he goes into the same bar every evening for twenty years and has two drinks. One night he goes into the bar as usual, has two drinks, and pees on the bar. OK the barman overlooks it. This guy's been coming here for twenty years. Next night. The same. Two drinks and pees on the bar. The barman says: 'Go see my cousin Herman. He's a psychiatrist. He'll sort you out.' He disappears for six months. Then comes back and says to the barman: 'I've been to see your cousin Herman. He sorted me out.' Has two

drinks and pees on the bar. 'I thought you said
my cousin Herman sorted you out?' 'Yes. I know
why.'

Me   what's the why of all this Watergate business?

He   Watergate is an extreme left-wing conspiracy.
They are after him because they have never
forgiven him for getting Alger Hiss. Douglas is a
metastasis. But Nixon's next Supreme Court
appointment should secure things for the next
eighteen years.

Me   how about the trade unions? how infiltrated
(by metastases from extreme left-wing cancer)?

He   they are still quite wholesome. We arranged a
strike recently.

Me   between?

He   Union leadership and Management. Gives a good
impression to the membership that the leadership
is strong. They like to feel it's strong. I don't
see any extreme left-wing takeover in the unions.

Me   maybe Kissinger is a communist agent

He   you never can tell these days. The CIA is
infiltrated with communists. You have to have a
very suspicious mind to follow the moves these
days.
I've read Marx. There's a lot in what he says.
He would be right if people were idealists.
But that's not the nature of the beast.
(two more of the same)
the newspapers, TV: they are all infiltrated.
Do you know that *Time* and *Newsweek* have been
bought up by the extreme left wing?

Me   have you been to China?

He   no. I'm still suspicious of China. But we exchange
scientific information. They are right there in
analytical chemistry. Twenty years ahead of the
Russians. We're just marketing a pill that's about
six years behind the one they have had out for
some time. How do they do it when they are so
cut off!!

Me   maybe they think we're cut off

He	the trouble with Americans is that they are so self-destructive. We licked the Japs and the Germans. Then let ourselves be taken advantage of. The trouble was Potsdam. Roosevelt was senile and surrounded by extreme left-wing infiltrators. (pause for mutual reflection) have you read Tolkien?
Me	no
He	he's behind a lot of the way young people's minds are working. I can't make head or tail of him.

Feb. 1973, Harrison Hot Springs

Masseur	Yes, Mr . . .
Laing	Laing (as in *ang*-el)
Masseur	Lang, Mr Lang (as in gang) right we are (starts massage, stops, goes to appointment book, spells out L-A-I-N-G, comes back) you're not R. *D*. Lang
Laing	R. D. *Laing*
Masseur	you're not R. D. *Lang*
Laing	R. D. *LAING*
Masseur	you're not R. D. *LANG* the writer? (the massage becomes unpleasant and gets more so to the end)
Laing	as a matter of fact, I suppose I have to say I am
Masseur	no you're not. This is no laughing matter. (pause) no you are not
Laing	(I have been face down – I turn around on one elbow and say to him menacingly) I am not asking you to believe me (pause; silence; I lie down again – massage continues in cold silence)
Masseur	(quivering through his effort to 'watch it') what are you doing this weekend?
Laing	(I had to make a decision. I decided I would

                    go on with this up to a point, but felt too
                    vulnerable face down, so I turned over.)
                    that'll do for that; just a little this way
Masseur   what are you doing this weekend?
Laing   I'm doing a workshop
Masseur   where?
Laing   in Vancouver
Masseur   it's not in Vancouver
Laing   I don't know where it is, somewhere around
                    there
Masseur   I wanted to go but they said I wasn't qualified
Laing   I'm sorry
Masseur   and I couldn't afford the fees
                    (it's getting worse:
                    he hates me if I'm *not* R. D. Laing,
                                    for leading him on
                    and he hates me if I am . . .)
Laing   (mutters) I've been here before
Masseur   pardon
Laing   nothing
                    (pause)
Masseur   how do I know you're R. D. LANG?
Laing   that's not my problem
Masseur   (pleading – menacingly) R. D. Lang wrote books
Laing   have you read any?
Masseur   no
Laing   I wrote *The Divided Self, Self and Others,
                    Sanity, Madness and the Family, The Politics of
                    Experience, Knots, The Politics of* . . .
                    (He does not recognize any of them)
Masseur   R. D. LANG wrote *The Bird of Paradise*
Laing   I wrote *The Bird of Paradise*
                    (silence)
                    (He may kill me)
Masseur   are you a doctor?
Laing   yes
Masseur   a *real* doctor?
Laing   yes
                    (silence – massage ends
                    I am putting on robe to go)

Masseur	(suddenly) I have to kill time here so I wanted to learn English literature; I was going to start with Gertrude Stein and you, and someone else I can't remember
Laing	Shakespeare?
Masseur	I can't remember. What do you think?
Laing	The Bible and Shakespeare – that's what I was brought up on
Masseur	so what do you think?
Laing	what do you want to study English literature for?
Masseur	to improve my mind
Laing	well er I'm sorry I have to go now, Cheerio
Masseur	what do you think?

Oct. 1974, On the train from London to Scotland

Getting pissed at the bar with sundry 'other' ranks from a Scottish regiment.
(round of drinks)

Me	Ireland must be tough
1st Soldier	the worst thing about Ireland, you know what it is?
Me	tell me
1st Soldier	while you're there you're restricted to two pints of beer a day and when you come back
2nd Soldier	you lash out
3rd Soldier	you blow it
1st Soldier	it's normal isn't it
2nd Soldier	it's natural
3rd Soldier	it's fuckin inevitable (round of drinks)
1st Soldier	my ambition in life, you know what it is?
Me	tell me
1st Soldier	find a white woman and a black man in bed and put a grenade between them (general round of applause and approval) (round of drinks)
2nd Soldier	look at him
3rd Soldier	he's fuckin looking fuckin miserable

4th Soldier	Aye why not?
2nd Soldier	didn't you shoot your load in London?
4th Soldier	oh aye, this morning
2nd Soldier	and you've got a missus waiting for you?
Me	does she know you're on your way?
4th Soldier	I haven't told her I'm coming
	(general sympathetic laughter and shaking of heads)
	(round of drinks)
4th Soldier	if I catch her with a man
Me	kill him or beat her up?
4th Soldier	beat her up definitely. definitely. Fuck it definitely.
A Sailor	why should it be any different for her?
1st Soldier	it's fuckin different mate
2nd Soldier	you just shoot your load and you're off
	(general assent)
1st Soldier	she opens her legs
4th Soldier	that's it
2nd Soldier	she receives it. You just shoot your load.
Sailor	still we do it, why shouldn't they?
1st Soldier	there's no right and wrong
4th Soldier	I'm no angel
Me	no one suggested you were
2nd Soldier	it's different for a woman
Sailor (to 4th Soldier)	you should have married a man
1st Soldier	Aw fuck
2nd Soldier	maybe
4th Soldier,	it's not so simple
	(another round)
Sailor	they're another species
	they're another fuckin species

Epilogue

Plato's dialogue *The Parmenides** ends this way

Parmenides Let thus much be said; and further let us affirm
what seems to be the truth, that, whether one is
or is not, one and the others in relation to themselves and one another, all of them, in every way,
are and are not, and appear to be and appear
not to be.

Aristoteles Most true.

One is coerced in the movement of the dialogue
to agree with Aristoteles to this, I find most disquieting,
conclusion, since one is forced either to jump off by denying
the validity of one's own thought or, continuing to think, to be
forced to a conclusion my thought, at least, does not like.

David Hume and a few others seem to have had
or to have the equanimity to propose that it comes to the
choice of a false reason or none at all.

In whatever event, if one *thinks* about what is
the case and what is not the case seriously, intensely, and long
enough, one seems either to drive oneself insane or to come
to the conclusion that almost everyone else is or that we all
are, when it comes down to it, one might say, metaphysically.

A few hard-headed Scotsmen (Reid and others –
the philosophers of common sense)† insisted that even if our
thinking can lead us up a garden path paved by logical
consistency into metaphysical nightmare, spiritual hell, moral

---

* Jowett translation.
  † S. A. Grave, *The Scottish Philosophy of Common Sense*, Oxford
University Press, London 1960.

nihilism, and a total intellectual débâcle in irresolvable paradoxes, nevertheless they were not abdicating *their* common sense.

However, I am unable to 'believe in', or 'trust', ultimately, my 'common sense', either. I wish I could, but I do not seem to be in control of these matters.

Yet 'behind', as it were, all this sort of thing, I have held for most of my life, and do so now, more than ever, certain – I'm not sure what best to call them – convictions? but authorized by what or whom?

God given? genetically – culturally determined? chosen? and if so, wishfully?

Nevertheless, however much I riddle them with my own riddles and sometimes ridicule, *they* do seem to determine, or at least affect, the direction of my life. I have become convinced of *that,* as an empirical fact, from my observation of both my life and others.

I serve values, not always faithfully or constantly, but I nevertheless feel *bound* to them, I can't get away from them. If I can't prove them right, I can't prove them wrong. They are not contrary to my common sense, though they often run counter to what seem to be my short-term interests, certainly my short-term inclinations.

But not to my long-term inclinations. I want to live correctly. To live correctly cannot be wrong. There *must* be a correct way to live. That way must conform to the nature of life, and to what is the case.

What *is* our environment?

Does what is, what is the case, include spiritual, emotional environments, which are not secondarily, tertiarily, or quaternally derived from our physical environment?

It is no use trying to split up and fragment the problem under the pretence that this is *analysing* the problem.

For example. Truth and lying.

Lying is one of the most underwritten about phenomena in psychology. Understandably, for a number of obvious reasons. There are many kinds of lies. Let me be more explicit.

In the course of my professional work as well as elsewhere I have come across something like this scenario often. It is so common, typologically, as to dissolve anyone's anxieties that they could be identified by it.

The simple story of sexual infidelity, deceit, jealousy, etc. The secret affair between a man and his wife's best friend. The (sometimes simultaneous) affair between a woman and her husband's best friend, married to her best friend.

If it is decided to follow the path of deception, as things go on, sometimes for years and years, an extraordinarily complex, intricate pattern of misrepresentations, equivocations, and outright lies has to have been woven, and kept up, with some measure of consistency.

Then a lady of seventy discovers that her husband has had a mistress for the last thirty years. That all her friends knew. Those business conferences! and all the usual rest of it. She is maybe jealous. But she is quivering, physically, because she says, and I have no reason to disbelieve her, her *whole sense of reality* has been shattered. Her mind runs through all those years: she discovers she has been shrouded in a tissue of deception, all those years. She is past being outraged. She feels desperate because she has been cheated of reality. She has been deprived of truth. I'm sure that truth deprivation can wreak as much havoc to some people as vitamin deprivation.

We *need* truth. Truth and reality seem sometimes virtually indistinguishable, sometimes separable, but always most intimately related.

What is the case must include my environment, and to live correctly, my genes need to know what is the case.

In the end, what determines in law whether someone is completely 'gone' or not is the answer to the question: Does he or she know the difference between right and wrong?

After practising 'psychiatry' for twenty-five years, I ought to have been able to come to some at least testable scientific hypotheses. Come across some facts that point in one direction or another.

But the facts seem to be pointable in many directions. They themselves seem largely dependent on us for the type/form of existence we take them to have.

It seems that they themselves cannot be our ultimate authority, since we, if we do not construct them entirely, as some have said, still seem unable not to construe them in some way or other not finally dictated by the facts themselves.

We come back to ourselves as our own final authority. But if we are as far, or as much, as we can appeal to, then many of the shrewdest of our fellows have refused to go farther than to say that though we ourselves are all we have to go on, we may ourselves be so limited and/or even so deranged, that as media for truth, we have not a snowball's chance in hell.

Words attributed to reputed spiritual, religious, intellectual world figures attribute to us, sometimes to themselves as well, gross ignorance, confusion, spiritual darkness, innate moral depravity, etc., etc.

Opinions vary as to whether such is the state of affairs. If it is, is it remediable? If remediable, by human effort or by the grace of God, if there is a God, alone?

In this morass, I feel like a disoriented blind bat sinking into quicksand, without even being able to feel gleeful in the assurance that anyone is in a better position.

yet 'Surely beyond that last blue ridge of mountains rimmed with snow.

dwells a man who knows why men are born?'

What is?

They have been married four years. And have only one child. He has been studying spiritual-mental disciplines of Northern India and Tibet. Is particularly drawn to the tantric world.

He has affairs with other women. In particular, *an* other woman, whom he has staying with them.

As his wife enters the sitting room one afternoon there they are on the sofa.

'It's too much! I can't stand it! Get that woman out of the house,' she yelled.

'That's not a woman,' he replied, referring to the
object beside him, on the sofa,
            'that's a waterfall.'

        I don't know whether I've got a problem at all
that's what I've come to see you about
                to cut a long story short
            It's my six-year-old daughter she was doing
very badly at school she was behind with her reading and
writing and arithmetic and she was insufferable to me wouldn't
do anything I asked her I could do nothing with her and then
about two months ago butter wouldn't melt in her mouth and
suddenly she was reading, and writing, and top in her class
in arithmetic I knew something was up and I asked her what
had come over her and she said 'Nothing mummy' but I
knew she was lying so I got it out of her I couldn't believe it I
just couldn't believe it she was having an *affair* with my husband her father she was sucking his penis every
other day and they were carrying on like that under my
very roof I asked her why she hadn't told me and she said
'I didn't want to upset you mummy' and I can't tell the police
because I love him and she would never forgive me and now
he's having an affair with her best friend and I think the whole
class is starting to queue up what do you think? when I
challenged him he just asked me to join them then I thought
this is probably what I wanted to do with my father if I had
done that with my father I wouldn't be all screwed up like I
am now very likely. I wish he had been my daddy. do you
think there is a problem?

        Moonlight plays on a silver stream in the jungle.
        The young man has a commanding presence:
gentle, charming, reserved, handsome. His devotees are all
Indians. They take him to be Mahavatar Babaji.
        A cultured old Indian lady is telling me of her
meetings with Babaji, as he sits next to her, inclining his head
attentively.
        She had met Babaji three times in her life. This
third time, she is an old woman and he, the young man we

are sitting with. Last time, about thirty years ago, they were both in middle age. And the first time was a long, long time ago, when he was a very old man, and she, a very young girl.

There is a professor of chemistry at Banaras.
He specializes in laser research.
He told me that while pursuing his researches in Japan, an Indian gentleman, dressed in a dhoti, came into his laboratory.
He told the professor to return to Banaras to continue his research. There was no further conversation.
They walked to the door of the laboratory. His visitor put a hand on his shoulder, and disappeared into thin air.
The professor went immediately to his Japanese colleague, with whom he was engaged in research, told him of the visit, and that he would have to wind up his work there and return to India.
This was accepted without demur, and he returned to Banaras where his research continues.

A friend of mine told me he had asked a Tibetan tulku, reputed to be a Bodhisattva, whether or not he believed the stories of a wonder-working Indian guru, who seems to produce sophisticated pieces of matter out of the air.
The Tibetan replied: 'I don't know whether to believe that sort of thing or not.'
My friend was nonplussed, because he thought that someone of the Tibetan's spiritual station *should* know whether to believe 'that sort of thing' or not.
When I told this story to another friend of mine who is as knowledgeable about reputed sages all over the place as anyone I know, he evinced no surprise. 'That's the type of mind they have cultivated.'
In many conversations in India, between culti-vated, educated people, it was evident to me that there was a profound (but not that easy to see or express clearly) differ-ence in how we took things to be. For them (allow a reckless

generalization) anything was possible. Under usual circumstances, there was a high antecedent probability that certain
things would happen, or that they would not. But the conscious
beyond consciousness of the holy man is at one with the One
and All, wherein *all* possibilities reside. Not just our
predictions. Man proposes, God disposes.

A Christian theologian said to me, it's not a
question of what God *can* do, it's a question of what he *does* do.

When I was fourteen, I was asked what I wanted
to study when I was older. I replied without hesitation:
'Psychology, philosophy, and theology.' I was quickly in
disgrace when I would not give more than the foggiest
account of what each of these terms meant.
Let us say that psychology is the study of the
psyche, philosophy is the love of wisdom, and theology an
attempt to articulate the relation of creation to the divine.
Most people called psychologists today probably
don't believe that a psyche exists, except as the manifestation
of certain physical functions, many present-day philosophers
believe that all but a very few of their predecessors were
disastrously wrong in their methods and conclusions, and
many present-day theologians would be regarded by almost
all their predecessors as heretics and/or atheists.
By the time I was seventeen, the philosophers I
had read arrived, each more or less convincingly and per-
suasively, at what seemed incompatible contradictions between
them. There was no consensus. Human beings the world over
regarded by millions as sages taught diverse doctrines
including the doctrine of no doctrine. So in psychology and
theology everyone differed. How could us newcomers decide
right from wrong, truth from falsity? The very nature of what
was a fact was up for grabs.
I abandoned everything else and took to science.
Not what science might at any time present us with as, provisionally, fact, but the scientific *method*. Here at least the
human mind had arrived at a way of proceeding which, if it

perhaps could never solve the riddle of the universe, common sense schooled to the sharpness of sagacity, might reconcile us to the necessary disenchantment at resigning ourselves, more or less gracefully, to our limitations.

However, although I thought I wanted to study embryology, and neurophysiology in particular, I found that I could not keep away from psychoanalysis. From the start, I had grave misgivings as to whether psychoanalysis was a science, since I doubted that it proceeded by a scientific *method*. But my fascination overruled my qualms, and I have found that, despite myself, it has been over matters psychological, philosophical, and theological that my mind has pondered through the years. Often with a most unpleasant sense of the vanity of such pondering.

Let me go back to some words, as an example of the problem I am trying to express.

A strong resonance in the word from which 'to sin' is translated is 'to miss the mark', in archery, to be 'off' target. Even if this is not the only note in the complex chord of this word, it changes for me the quality of the sense of the word I grew up with in my immediate Scottish Presbyterian culture. It aligns the term to such terms as 'error', such expressions as 'to err [to sin?] is human, to forgive divine'.

Kierkegaard made it clear to me that contrition was not what I thought 'guilt' was.

'Give us each day our daily bread.' 'Daily' is a translation of a Greek word, literally meaning 'superessential'.

An old New Testament scholar assures me that 'Who is not for you is against you' is a wrong translation; it ought to read: 'Who is not against you is for you'.

And so on. Not only the trustworthiness of the most authentic earliest MS is disputed, but the translations therefrom.

To investigate one of any such matters at first hand one has to devote a full lifetime, and even then would not stand a chance of holding an opinion worth having on innumerable issues of complex scholarship without an exceptionally fine intellect and very rare qualities of character.

In every field, the field itself is so vast that to be a good all-rounder in just one speciality deserves respect.

Nevertheless, there is still the fallacy of not being able to see the woods for the trees. Difficult if one is oneself a tree in the woods, not even one of the tallest. Difficult if there is no vantage point outside the woods, from which to survey the woods.

It seems to be incontrovertible that someone said that someone said that he was the way, the truth, and the life. And that in that capacity he promised that whenever two or three people were gathered together in the name of the Way, the Truth, and the Life, there 'I' am in the midst.

Even if we do not know the way or cannot believe that there *is* a way, even if we don't know the truth or don't believe that there is *the* truth, and even if life with a capital L seems mumbo jumbo, if in the name of these matters we still come together, then 'I', which is not the hallucinations we have inside each of our sacks of skin, is in our midst.

That seems to me a most profound proposition.

Dare I believe it? Dare I not?

This book is haunted by the question: What is the correct way to live? When I put this question, through an interpreter, to a reputed saint in Kashmir, said to be over a hundred years old (he looked like an ancient bird), the instant answer, through the interpreter, was:

Let your heart be like the sun
Shine alike on everyone.

Whence did he derive this knowledge? Or was it mere opinion?

'The scientific and technical world of modern man,' writes C. F. von Weizsäcker, 'is the result of his daring enterprise, knowledge without love.'* Chilling. I cannot see how knowledge without love can yield knowledge of love; how a heartless method, yielding heartless results, can do anything else than explain *away* the heart.

Werner Heisenberg, in an address given on the Pnyx hill in Athens in 1964,† after a searching probe into our

* *The History of Nature*, University of Chicago Press, Chicago, 1949, p. 190.

† 'Natural Law and the Structure of Matter', The Rebel Press, London, 1970, pp. 44. 45. The English version is by Heisenberg.

capacity to 'understand' the world mathematically, suggests that 'patterns in our minds', called archetypes by Plato, may 'reflect the internal structure of the world' in ways mathematics cannot. 'Whatever the explanation of these other [than mathematical] forms of understanding may be, the language of the images, metaphors and similes, is probably the only way to approach the ''one'' from wider regions.'

'You Scottish theologians,' a Swiss theologian once said to me, 'just tell stories. You do not theologize.' Parables however may be the only way, sometimes.

This book makes no pretensions to be a guide to the perplexed. I am myself perplexed. But I have tried, as best I can, to convey the nature of my perplexity.

Can what is morally wrong be scientifically right? Two worlds shatter each other.

Toward the end of his life, C. G. Jung had the nerve to write: 'We must completely give up the idea of the psyche being somehow connected with the brain . . . '*

I am sure he was not suffering from senile dementia, nor was it a slip of the pen, or an ill-considered statement.

To Lévi-Strauss and many others, Bergson, Sartre, and, I would imagine, Jung are prime examples of 'savage minds' in our twentieth-century civilized midsts. In 1913, Albert Schweitzer undertook a psychiatric study of Jesus, and against the opinion of a number of eminent psychiatrists concluded that there was insufficient evidence to pronounce him insane.

However, he could give him the benefit of the doubt only by discounting much of what he seemed to mean, and by culturally relativizing his world view.

St Catherine of Siena is credited with the remark:
All the way to Heaven
     is Heaven.
For has He not said,
     I am the Way?

* 'Synchronicity', in *The Interpretation of Nature and the Psyche*, Pantheon, New York, 1955, p. 123.